Chloe Giordano

NEEDLEPAINTED
WOODLAND ANIMALS

First published in 2024

This book is an expanded paperback edition of
The Embroidered Art of Chloe Giordano, first published in 2019

Search Press Limited
Wellwood, North Farm Road,
Tunbridge Wells, Kent TN2 3DR

Suppliers

If you have any difficulty obtaining any of the materials or equipment mentioned in this book, then please visit the Search Press website for details of suppliers: www.searchpress.com

Bookmarked Hub

For further ideas and inspiration, and to join our free online community, visit www.bookmarkedhub.com

Find Chloe
- at: www.chloegiordano.com
- on Instagram: @chloegiordano_embroidery
- on Facebook: chloegiordanoillustration

DEDICATION

For Mum and Vince.

ACKNOWLEDGEMENTS

With thanks to the team at Search Press, and to everyone who has assisted me on my embroidery journey.

MIX
Paper | Supporting responsible forestry
FSC® C144853
www.fsc.org

Chloe Giordano

NEEDLEPAINTED
WOODLAND ANIMALS

Exquisite embroidered art

SEARCH PRESS

Contents

Introduction

Unlike a lot of embroiderers, I do not come from a crafty background and I did not learn to stitch at home. Instead, I had intended to become an illustrator in more conventional mediums: I studied Illustration at the University of the West of England in Bristol, working with pencils and oil paints for the majority of my degree. It was in my final year that I became interested in the world of textile art (especially after watching Michel Gondry's wonderful film, *The Science of Sleep*), and began experimenting with fabric in my own work.

I fell in love with the tactile nature of thread and fabric. I started to learn traditional embroidery stitches, and began creating my first textile designs, making soft, abstract sculptures. However, I found myself missing the realistic elements of my old illustration work, and felt as though I was drifting away from my visual goals. I started to use sewing thread in the same way I would use paint – freehand, following the flow of the subject and making decisions as I went. After a lot of trial and error I arrived at my current needle-painting technique, which I hope succeeds in bridging the gap between embroidery and painting, but this method is always changing and evolving. In this updated paperback edition I will be sharing how I've continued to explore what is possible in this medium.

The natural world has always been important to me and remains a vital component of my work. Originally from Buckinghamshire, England and having lived in Oxfordshire for a few years, I relocated up north to Yorkshire, where I have the convenience of being near a city while also having having easy access to the countryside that inspires so many of my embroideries. I am endlessly fascinated and touched by the fragility of our wildlife here in Britain, and I have spent countless hours studying, drawing and embroidering these animals. I hope I have managed to capture at least some of their magic.

Equipment & materials

Almost all my embroidery materials can be found in any craft shop on the high street or main street, or online. I discovered most of my favourite art materials at university while working on traditional illustration. As is true for many disciplines, I worked through a range of methods and equipment before settling on what worked best for me.

. . . .

SKETCHBOOK

I have been using unlined Moleskine® notebooks as sketchbooks for years. As the paper is thinner than the traditional Moleskine® sketchbooks, they hold twice as much paper. This does mean that you can often see drawings through the paper, but this does not bother me: I use my sketchbooks as a place to record ideas and work through my thought process – I am not concerned with how pretty they look!

PENCILS

I am loyal with my pencils and use only two – Mars® Lumograph® B by Staedtler, and Palomino 602 Blackwing by Blackwing®. They both allow you to go from light, controlled marks to very dark ones, so you can achieve a lot of contrast in a small area. The Blackwing is softer, so I tend to use it for loose sketches where I am just throwing ideas around; I then switch to the Lumograph to capture finer details and create my final reference drawing.

PAINTS

I use gouache paints in the same sketchbook as my drawings, as they work in concert with my drawings. Gouache is very similar to watercolours but is more opaque; this allows me to layer up colours over dried paints, helping me see which concentration of colour I prefer. This is especially useful when I am deciding how much dye I want to wash into my background fabric.

BRUSHES

When it comes to paint brushes I am not picky! It is usually a case of shuffling through my cupboard of art supplies and seeing what falls out.

OTHER ART MATERIALS

Rather than scissors, I like to use a craft knife to cut out designs to use as 'silhouettes', or templates. This is simply because they are more precise and cut cleaner lines. (See page 28 for more information on this.) I use the knife with a cutting mat, to protect my working surface.

SEWING THREAD

Using sewing thread rather than embroidery thread/floss allows much more detail to be packed into a small area. It also saves the trouble of having to separate out single strands of embroidery thread/floss.

EMBROIDERY THREAD/FLOSS

I only use embroidery thread/floss to back my work. It is stronger than sewing thread, and so I trust it to hold the back of the fabric together for a long time. I usually use DMC.

FABRIC

I use unbleached calico for most of my work, which I dye by hand. I like calico because it has a high enough thread count to allow for a lot of detail, but it is also sturdy enough to support being heavily embroidered. I also find its texture, which is slightly rougher than standard cotton, more interesting for backgrounds, and I will purposely iron it while still wet to give it a parchment-like texture. Prior to stitching, I always wash my fabric to remove any substances from the surface and to prevent shrinkage later on.

NEEDLES

I use size 12 sewing needles, which are the smallest I have managed to find. This size allows for plenty of detail to be worked and can pass through areas where there is already a lot of thread packed in. The downside is that they are very prone to bending and breaking. I buy them in large batches and replace them as soon as they start to bend.

THIMBLE

I use a thimble to protect the fourth finger of my right hand, as this is the one I use to push the needle through the fabric. Not everyone needs to use a thimble, but I would recommend it when working with very small needles: the eye end is so small that it can pierce the skin if you put a lot of pressure on it.

SCISSORS

I have only one pair of fabric scissors and one pair of embroidery scissors. I freely admit I picked my embroidery scissors for the design, not for functionality, but they work well!

EMBROIDERY HOOP

I use wooden hoops as I can then sand and stain them myself, depending on the design. I like to work in a hoop several times larger than the embroidery, so I have room to organize the threads I am working with. When preparing the fabric for the embroidery hoop, it is important to stretch it until it is fully taut, and with the hoop tightened as much as possible, or you will end up with areas of loose fabric around the embroidery (see also page 26). You will need to keep tightening the fabric and hoop as you embroider, as the fabric does eventually become loose again. To make sure my fabric and hoop are ready to use for embroidering, I tap the fabric with my fingers – if it feels like the surface of a drum, it is good to go.

AIR-ERASABLE (VANISHING) FABRIC MARKER

I use vanishing fabric markers to draw in the main outlines of the design on to the fabric, prior to stitching. The markers are water-soluble but the marks will also disappear on their own in a couple of days, which I prefer to let them do. The only downside to these pens is that using them repeatedly on the same bit of fabric can cause it to stain, which is why I will always stitch the outline of a design when I know it will take me longer than a day or two to complete. Then I use the pen within each section to draw and define the more complicated details. When using a very dark fabric, like black cotton, I use tailor's chalk.

FABRIC DYE

I use powder dyes so that I can mix them and create the specific colours I need. I vary how long I leave the fabric in the dye and will often do several washes to achieve the colour I want. The only exception to this is when I want to work on a solid black background – this cannot be achieved with powder dye on calico, so I use black cotton instead. I use mostly Dylon® dyes, as they are easy to blend together and create customized shades and colours.

Inspiration

I have always been fascinated by animals. I have been drawing and painting them my whole life, so they are a natural choice to use as the main subjects of my embroideries.

. . . .

Mostly, I prefer to depict wild animals because they feel like more mysterious, romantic subjects than domesticated animals. There are a lot of myths and folk tales about wildlife, especially where I live in Britain, and these are always interesting areas to explore for ideas.

Natural history has been a big source of inspiration for me, and if I am not sure what to create next, I will spend a couple of hours in one of the natural-history museums to get some ideas flowing. Taking along a sketchbook and spending some time drawing the preserved animals I see on display can be a nice change of scenery from embroidering at home.

Another option a bit closer to home is looking at nature guides and books on natural history, and I have a stack of them that I have steadily collected over the years. As well as using them to check physical and anatomical details, guides can offer an insight into how to lay out a subject of a nature-based design: older editions tend to rely more heavily on traditional illustrations, rather than photographs, and can make for more inspiring viewing with their ornate, stylized depictions of the creatures described.

Composing an image

I spend a lot of time in my sketchbook before moving on to an embroidery. I use this time to work through ideas, and to try to figure out what will be the best approach to each piece before committing anything to thread.

• • • • • • • • • •

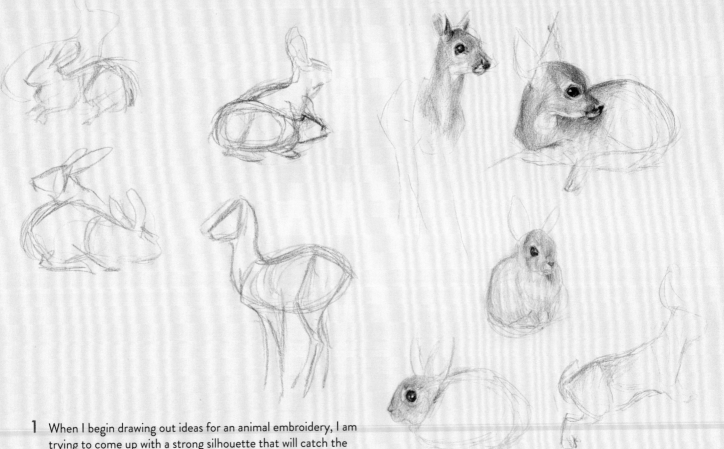

1 When I begin drawing out ideas for an animal embroidery, I am trying to come up with a strong silhouette that will catch the eye. At this point I am not looking to do a good drawing, but just to quickly jot down ideas that are dynamic and capture the movement and posture of the animal. I use these loose sketches to play around with different compositions for the same piece too.

2 Once I have found an idea I like, I will do a few focused
drawings from reference photographs to gain an
understanding of how the animal is formed and how it moves.
I concentrate on any areas I am unsure of, like how a leg
bends or what muscles are carrying the animal's weight.
These drawings are a bit tidier than my original sketches,
but are still just a means to an end – to understand what I'm
wanting to embroider. I never directly copy a photograph
with my embroidery, partly because this would violate the
photographer's copyright of the original image, but also
because I have never seen a photograph that was ready to
be embroidered without anything being reworked. A nice
photograph does not always equal a good embroidery.

*I love embroidering eyes, so I always
do a few drawings just to commit the
details to memory.*

3 After these studies, I move on to a final drawing that I will then
work from as I embroider. As well as making a visually pleasing
image, I use this drawing to pin down what details I wish to
include, and to work out the directions my stitches will go in.
 This stage is especially important if the subject is in a more
compact position, like lying down, as more parts of the animal
are intersecting and this means I have to decide how to manage
the 'colliding' areas of fur.

This final drawing does not have to be the only drawing I work from though. Sometimes I will have another go at drawing an element, such as the head, if I am still feeling a bit unsure about how to portray it; I then flick between these drawings and my main reference sketch as I embroider. If I am really struggling with a section of the embroidery, I will go back to my sketchbook and use a pencil to work out ways to lay down the stitches until I know how to move forward.

· · · · · · · · · · ·

Thinking about colour

I always try to think about colour before I begin a new piece, rather than making it up as I go along. Learning how to blend colours together when embroidering takes practice, but will be much easier if you have carefully picked out the threads you want to use beforehand.

. . . .

• • • • • • • • • • •

I normally have a strong idea of what colours I want to use
from the beginning. If I am not sure whether certain colours
will go well together, I will do a small mock-up in paint to see
how it looks. If there are going to be complicated or confusing
colour changes, I make a digital painting on my computer of
the colours I would like to use (see 'White Rabbit' on pages
136–139) to help me stay on track. I use this more often for
background designs than for the animals themselves.

I use a wide variety of thread colours that I have been slowly collecting over the last few years. I seem to use around 8–12 colours for an animal embroidery, and background colours can vary in number too, depending on how much detail I have decided to include. I like to line up the spools on my desk in order of colour to make sure they go together, and will usually spend a few minutes swapping colours in and out until I make up my mind.

• • • • • • • • • •

Having a wide range of colours is important, but it is not the only thing to consider. I cannot mix colours with threads in the same way as I can with paint, so I need to rely on choosing colours that fit together well to capture the different tones and shades. I encourage you to think carefully about what each colour thread is for. I like to pick out the lightest and darkest tones first, based on my initial drawing, and then decide what colours will be used in the remaining parts of the embroidery.

Another thing to consider when choosing your thread colours is that, occasionally, a particular colour does not exist independently but can be created through the influence of the other colours surrounding it. This is clearest when I am trying to blend warm colours into cold, such as pink into blue. I often use a grey thread in instances like these to act as a 'bridge' between these conflicting tones. By itself, grey can seem flat and colourless, but when put between warm and cold colours it appears more like violet. This can sound a bit strange, but if you look at some colour wheels, you can often find grey at the centre where all the colours meet.

'Needle-painting' is a very apt name for this embroidery technique, as the method is more similar to painting than you might initially think. A lot of painters work by laying down colours they have already mixed next to each other that, by themselves, suggest gradually shifting colours and tones, rather than using the brush to mix them on the canvas. This is how I used to work when I used oil paints, and I take the same approach when embroidering – just on a much smaller scale.

. . . .

'White Fawn', 2017
An example of both subtle and stark colour contrasts in the fur. (See also page 100.)

'Goldfinch', 2018

This goldfinch has an interesting mix of colour shifts, from the subtle changes in the brown and cream feathering to the stark red and gold markings they're best known for. Although there's little blending between those colours and the black, I included darker reds and yellows next to the black areas so the transition wouldn't be too jarring.

. . . .

When blending in a new colour, I start by adding one or two stitches of the new thread in amongst the original, and slowly increase the amount as I progress. Knowing when to add in another colour is something I consider very early on in the design process, usually when creating the drawing for the piece and selecting my colour palette. However, I also occasionally like to work freehand and I enjoy the element of making it up as I go along, feeling my way through and going with what I think is right for the piece.

I like to try to pick colours that work well together and will catch the eye. I have colour combinations I am particularly fond of: I love putting bright reds, golds and greens on to blue backgrounds to make the colours pop. Sometimes, however, I use colours similar to the background so that I can put in a lot of detail, but then 'knock it back' a bit so that the eye does not get confused. For example, I might use various shades of blue thread on a similar blue fabric, so that I can pack in a lot of pattern without detracting from the animal, the main subject of the embroidery.

. . . .

'Springing Fox', 2017
(See page 78.)

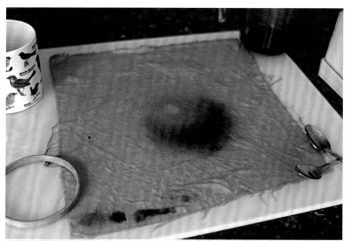

Hand-dyed fabric for 'Winter Blue Hare'
(See also pages 50–55.)

. . . .

Another way I like to play with colour is by dyeing my fabric. Not only does this allow me to achieve a shade that is hard to come by or impossible to find when buying calico, it also allows me to create subtle effects that complement and form part of the final embroidered design, as shown in 'Springing Fox', opposite.

Prior to dyeing, I plan out any colour shifts on the fabric when I am still working on the design in my sketchbook, as these will often play an important part in the overall composition. I start by laying out my square of chosen fabric on a protected surface, with my reference sketches nearby to give me guidance on where I will lay my dye. With a 15.25cm (6in) embroidery hoop close to me, to measure the necessary circumference of fabric to cover, I spoon some dye on to the fabric and spread it over the whole circle using the back of a spoon – this helps to control the direction of the dye.

While the first layer of dye is still wet, I spoon another volume of dye on to the fabric, this time around the bottom section of the circle to create a greater concentration of colour. Depending on the design, I will continue to add small amounts dye in the same way, slowly going darker and darker until I have achieved the effect I want. I let the dye soak in for about twenty minutes, then wash it off as usual. Depending on the embroidery, I also use a very diluted drop of bleach to create a light spot – a highlight. I always do this last, so I can wash the bleach off as quickly as possible.

Preparing the hoop

While embroidering, I normally work in a hoop several sizes larger than necessary,
such as a 15.25cm (6in) hoop. There are a few reasons for this.

. . . .

Using a larger hoop than necessary means that I can use the area around the
edge to store my threaded needles (see page 33, which explains a little more
about this). A larger hoop also means I worry less about accidentally marking
the fabric where I hold the hoop, or about permanent creases formed by the
hoop itself, because these held areas of fabric end up being cut off or tucked
away later on (see page 40). Finally, a large hoop also gives you more room
to manoeuvre as you embroider. If you used a hoop the same size as the
circumference of your finished embroidery, and you work right up to the edge
near the wood, it can become difficult to get the needle in and out as you may
keep hitting the frame by accident.

When putting the fabric in the hoop, I like to make sure it is completely taut
before beginning an embroidery. Once the fabric is lightly secured between
the two frames of the hoop, I tighten the screw repeatedly, tugging the edges
of the fabric all the way around as I go until I am left with a surface that is
tight and flat. Last of all, I like to push the inner hoop up so it is a millimetre
or two higher than the outer one, giving the embroidery a slightly raised
appearance. I find this helps hold the fabric steady.

I normally tap the fabric lightly to check it is ready to go – it should feel a bit
like tapping a drum.

Transferring the design

It is easy to waste a lot of time trying to transfer your detailed drawing on to fabric. For this reason, I have tried to find the quickest way to get the image transferred to the fabric, while staying as faithful as possible to the original drawing.

. . . .

1 Take your paper and place it over your chosen sketch. Rather than tracing paper, I tend to use ordinary paper (here, a piece torn from my sketchbook) that is sufficiently transparent to see the outline of my sketch.

2 Trace around your final drawing to create an outline.

3 Cut out your outline using a craft knife and cutting mat (or scissors, if that is easier for you).

4 Gently push out your silhouette from the paper.

5 Place the silhouette on your fabric. Draw around it with the air-erasable (vanishing) fabric marker.

6 Remove the silhouette to reveal your outline on the fabric.

7 Once the outline is in place, sketch in the essential details freehand – the eyes, contours of the legs and body and so on – using the initial drawing as a guide.

Starting to work

When beginning a new embroidery, I like to make sure I have everything
I might need to hand. Along with my needles, thread and scissors, I have my
sketchbook and any reference images beside me, so that I always have a clear
idea of how I want the final embroidery to look.

Saying that, when it comes to the embroidery process, I tend to work
freehand, so there is no exact plan for where I am going to put each stitch.
Although I do spend some time thinking about what colours to use before
I start, and how I want the thread direction to flow, often most of the final
placements are decided as I go. To me, this is the same way I would draw or
paint: although you can do practice sketches and plan how you want a piece to
look beforehand, most of the brush or pencil strokes are judgement calls that
you make as you work.

My methodology

Rather than moving around the embroidery, I prefer to start at one end and slowly stitch in a solid block as I work through the design. Some may wish to start with the body and try to stitch the head in the right place afterwards, but, from my own observations, most movement in animals starts with the head. For this reason, I begin at the very tip of the nose and follow the natural flow of the animal's body through the embroidery.

Although this method can make sticking to my original drawing more difficult – as my natural inclination is to stitch different areas of the design, to make sure everything is in the right place – this method of stitching from one side to the other helps to create the three-dimensional look I aim for. Moving back and forth and working over existing stitches would interrupt the flow of the piece, and break up the smooth appearance that progressive stitches make to create a more fur-like impression.

I like to pack my stitches together as tightly as possible, without too much overlapping. I find this is what gives my work a fluid, three-dimensional effect, as the stitches run together without criss-crossing over one other. The embroidery technique I use to achieve this is similar to the long-and-short stitch used in traditional embroidery, but I adjust the length of each stitch to fit the area and shaping I need to do: longer stitches are worked over areas where the animal's fur is stretched out, and shorter ones where it bunches together.

. . . .

• • • • • • • • • • •

Once I begin the embroidery, I thread up each colour as I need it. Once I finish using a particular shade I tend to keep it to the side of my work, even if I probably will not need it. I find this helps me to remember exactly what colours I have in play and how they look together.

To stop the threads getting tangled together at the back, I work the embroidery on the left-hand side of the hoop and pull the threads to the right-hand side, wrapping them over the edge of the frame and putting the needle back through the fabric so the thread is taut. The back of my work still becomes quite tangled and messy compared with most embroiderers' work, but as long as it does not hinder the stitching process, this does not bother me.

'Fawn'
2018

A typical piece will take me about forty hours to complete.
I use threads of about 30cm (12in) for ease of working: this means that they are neither too long, which would cause problems with tangling or knotting, nor too short, which would prevent the thread reaching easily over the work.

As you can see, I like to line up my threads in order of colour before I begin. This helps ensure they go well together, and it makes it easier to see the selection of colours with which I have chosen to 'paint' the creature.

· · · · · · · · · ·

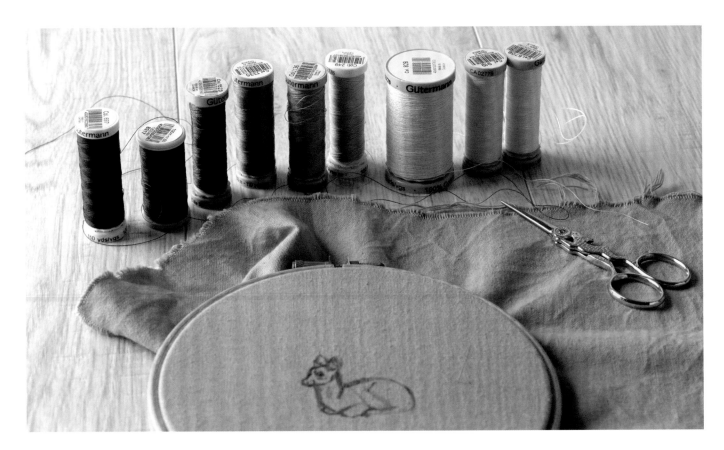

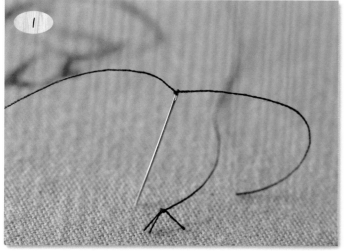

1 Thread the needle with your first thread: I tie a single knot at each end, one of which is through the eye of the needle to stop the thread from falling out.

2 I start to stitch the nose inside the drawn outline, bringing the thread up at one side of the nose and going back down on the other side.

3 I work several straight stitches of varying lengths to create the whole of the nose. Frequently check your embroidery against your initial reference drawing, so that you can make sure the two correspond and that you are happy with your stitch length and colour.

4 When you have finished working in your first colour, leave your thread 'parked' in the embroidery and change to the new thread and needle (see page 33). I prefer to keep all my colours threaded up in case I need them later – even if I am really sure I will not need a particular colour any more, I will still wait until the embroidery is further along before I tie it off. Especially at this stage in the embroidery, I like to try to avoid adding any more knots to extremely small areas like the nose and eye.

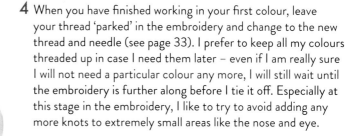

Tip

Starting inside the outline means that my embroidery ends up slightly smaller than the original drawing. This is because it is easier to add than to take away: if you start your piece too large, it is difficult to change this later. I have a tendency to under-stitch; more can always be added.

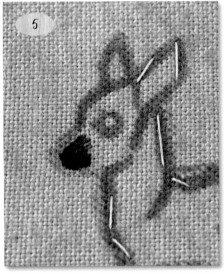

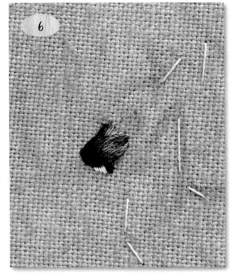

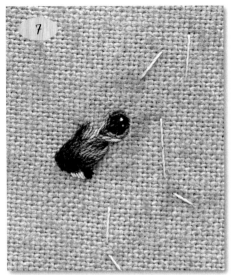

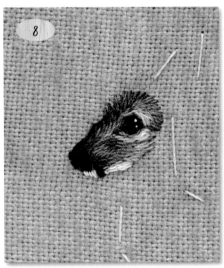

5 Before I continue with my stitching, I quickly work in the main outlines of the design in simple running stitch, as the pen marks will fade and I do not like to keep drawing over the same spots to avoid staining the fabric. I then begin to build up the threads and work outwards as I develop the fawn's muzzle, and slowly add new colours as needed.

6 At this point I work very slowly (even by my standards!), as it is very easy to make a mistake in such a small but important area. Always consider what every stitch is adding to the image.

7 Although it is tempting to add the eye highlights straight away, I try to wait until I have stitched the area around the eye too. If it is added too early, it can push up against the stitches making up the eye, distorting and changing the appearance of the highlight.

8 I continue to develop the head, paying particular attention to the shifts in colour around the eye as this part really brings the embroidery to life.

9 For me, this is the most difficult part of the embroidery: the ears. As I add these, I need to simultaneously keep them in line with the flow of stitches that make up the rest of the head.

10 I go on to complete the head and begin to work down the neck. This is where my original drawing becomes handy, as I use it to work out how I should change the direction of the fur.

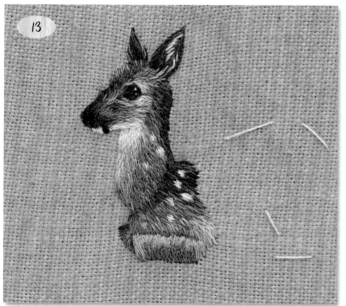

11 As I work down the neck, I begin to add in the fawn's white spots. I tend not to worry about sticking rigidly to my original drawing here, and just put them wherever works best with the rest of the stitching.

12 The neck now complete, I move on to the shoulders. As before, following my drawing carefully sees me through the change of thread direction.

13 When introducing the forelegs I try to keep in mind how real fur would behave, darkening it in places where it is tucked into the folds of skin, and adding highlights where it curves out and catches the light.

14 I add the remainder of the forelegs and begin developing the rest of the fawn's body. I keep referring to my initial drawing to make sure I am achieving the shifting tones and direction of the fawn's fur as accurately as possible.

15 I carefully change the thread direction and colour to depict the hindquarters. This is always a good place to push the darks and lights, and really make the embroidery pop.

16 I add in the hind leg and tail, finishing off the main design. I like to take a minute to look over the rest of the embroidery to see if there's anything that needs to be added or tidied up, but most of the time I manage to do everything as I go along!

17 Next, I move on to the background. I stitch a quick circle to show where the background will end. Once again I use a straight stitch for these details in the embroidery. The flowers are made up of very short stitches, which are turned in tight circles as I rotate the piece.

18 I had drawn out a design for the background, but – as with the fawn's spots – I do not stick to the preliminary sketch completely. I prefer to design the flora around the fawn embroidery, and improvise as I go until I am happy.

Finishing an embroidery

There are several options for displaying a finished embroidery,
the most popular being in a hoop. When choosing a hoop to display
a finished embroidery, I always like to have a gap of around
2.5cm (1in) between the hoop and the edge of the embroidery,
as this gives the design room to breathe.

. . . .

Instead of gluing the excess fabric to the back, I create a kind of drawstring
effect. Embroideries can loosen over time, so if this does occur the drawstring
stitches can simply be undone and tightened, and then drawn back together for an
embroidery that is taut once more.

When the embroidery is complete, I begin by cutting around it freehand,
leaving about 5cm (2in) of excess material around the edge. You are looking for
enough fabric to fold neatly to the back of the hoop. Using embroidery thread/floss
knotted twice at the end, I work large running stitches all the way around
the edge of the cut fabric. I then pull the thread/floss tight and knot it off. Finally,
I trim the end of the thread/floss, taking care to leave a short tail in case the work
ever needs to be loosened again. The excess thread/floss can then be tucked neatly
behind the folds of fabric.

I sell most of my work in hoops as this is how most people expect to see an
embroidery presented, but I actually prefer having them professionally framed. This
is because having a piece under glass will protect it from dust or any other debris
collecting on the surface of the embroidery, and to an extent it will protect it from
light damage too (although it is also important to hang an embroidery where it will
not be in direct sunlight). Most framers can provide glass that has an anti-reflection
coating on it, which reduces light glare and makes it less obvious that there is a layer
of glass between the viewer and the embroidery.

You could also turn smaller pieces into brooches or pendants. There are many
types of fittings available online, and these come with instructions on what size to
work at and how to secure each piece into the fitting.

THE
Embroideries

Hares

Hares can be a little challenging to capture as they are very similar to rabbits, which I also explore a lot in my work (see page 112). However, I always try to keep in mind what separates the two: hares have longer, stronger legs and larger paws, along with a different eye colour. Mountain hares are my favourites to stitch because they have a beautiful coat that changes throughout the seasons, making them fascinating subjects that frequently provide me with inspiration.

· · · · · · · · · ·

'Hare'

2016

Finished in a 12.75cm (5in) hoop

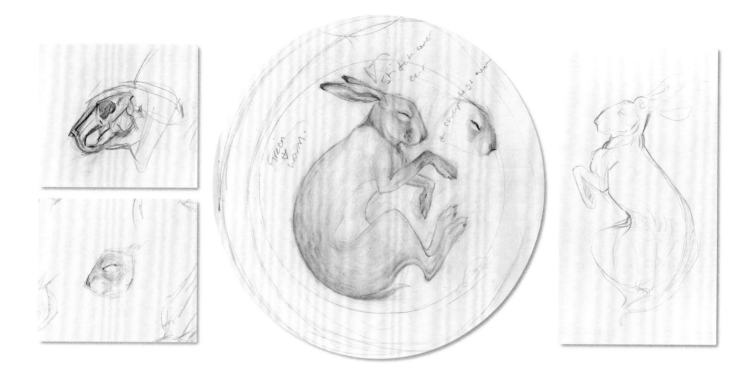

This was the first hare I embroidered. I wanted this hare to complement my earlier sleeping animals, but I struggled to find an image of a sleeping hare that captured the idea I had in my head. In the end, this pose was more from my imagination than reference, although I carefully pored over photos of rabbits in a similar position, spending time working out the bodily differences and how a hare would look instead.

. . . .

I struggled a lot with the planning stage of this embroidery, due to hares being an unfamiliar subject to me at the time. I erased and redrew the head several times until I was happy with how it looked.

At the last minute, I decided also to swap a mouse I had initially paired with the hare for a mushroom, in order to keep the design simpler and the focus on my main subject.

I hate to leave embroideries unfinished, so it did not cross my mind to give up on a piece that I was finding difficult! I think these situations are probably where I learn the most, so I will always see a challenging embroidery as an opportunity to improve.

Once again, upon beginning the embroidery, I struggled with the design. In fact, I wound up unpicking and restarting this piece several times, keen to capture the shape and expression of the sleeping hare I had sketched. In the photograph above, you can see one of the failed attempts to the right of the main embroidery, left in while I worked on the final piece so that I would remember what not to do!

. . . .

The reason I prefer to power through more complex embroideries, rather than give up if I think they are going badly, is because most of the time I get to the end and realize I was overcritical and the embroidery looks absolutely fine. Even now, during my working process, I nearly always have a moment when I think I have messed up an embroidery. However, these days I have learned to try to ignore the feelings of doubt and carry on.

This hare eventually went off to a gallery in the United States, so being able to complete it to a standard I was happy with was a relief! Now I had finished a sleeping hare, I felt prepared and ready to move on to the next challenge of embroidering an awake and active one.

. . . .

Throughout the process of stitching the hare, I made sure I emphasized the size of his paws – much larger than those of a rabbit – in addition to his striking facial profile.

ꙮ 'Summer Blue Hare' ꙮ

2016

Finished in a 10cm (4in) hoop

. . . .

I am most often drawn to mountain hares, known
also as blue hares, when choosing a particular species for my
embroidery. They are slightly smaller than the European hare
and their coats change colour in winter to a paler colour, to
camouflage them against the snow.

❧ 'Winter Blue Hare' ❧
2016

Finished in a 10cm (4in) hoop

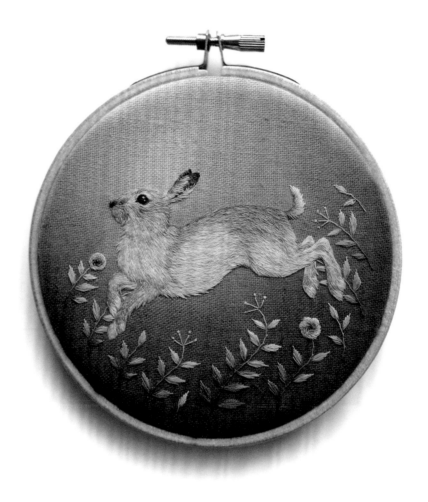

· · · · · · · · · ·

These two designs were deliberately created to partner with one another, to show the typical summer and winter coats of mountain hares.

I put a few hours of work into my sketchbook for these pieces, trying to create images that caught the hares leaping, the motion suspended. I also tried to stay aware of the unique appearance of hares, so I did not accidentally draw a rabbit!

plant,
near white,
darker background.

I tried to keep in mind the first sketch I made of the Summer Blue Hare as I worked on his winter counterpart, particularly concentrating on how I had drawn features like the nose and eye, so I could mimic them in this design.

· · · · · · · · · · ·

These two pieces mark the first time I experimented with using fabric dyes to create multiple tones rather than just one solid colour for the background.

To begin with, I dyed the squares of fabric a light blue. Then, while they were still wet, I began to add concentrated amounts of the same dye on to the fabric, slowly going darker and darker until I had the effect I wanted. I let the dye soak in for about twenty minutes, then rinsed it off as usual.

As they were a duo, the fabrics for both pieces were dyed at the same time, so I could use the same batch of blue dye and keep the backgrounds similar to one another. However, I varied the concentration of dye on each one to create slightly different effects and to allow each embroidery to be self-contained too.

· · · · · · · · · · ·

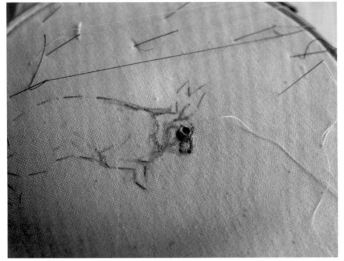

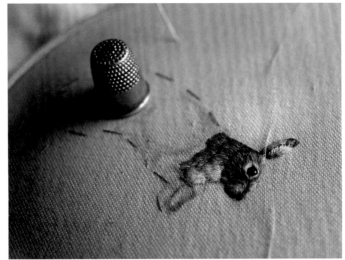

For the summer coat of this hare I kept mostly to soft browns, but also used white and cream threads for lighter patches of fur and to speckle through the rest of the coat. This helped show a suggestion of the hare's winter colours, waiting to come through.

Unlike the winter hare's background, here I kept the plants quite dark so that they would not contrast with the fabric too much, giving the overall piece a softer look – perfect for summer.

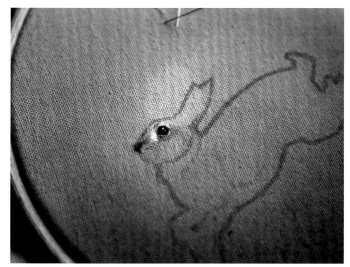

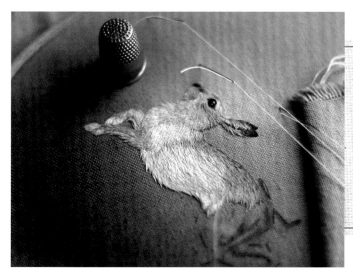

While working on a light-coloured animal, I had to resist the urge to use my usual darker threads for the tones in the fur near the colour contrast (where the body of the hare naturally contours and creates areas in shadow). Instead, before I started my embroidery, I chose a light brown thread and made sure I never went any darker than that.

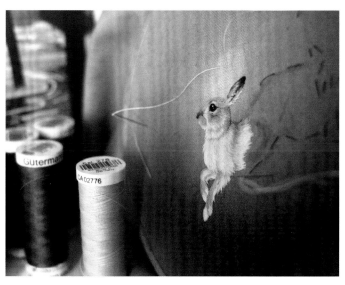

Finished in 10cm (4in) hoops

My favourite species of hare – the mountain hare – inspired me to
create another embroidered duo, this time with a navy background
and a slightly sober message.

At the time of working on this design, I had been reading a lot about the status of mountain hares on grouse moors. The hares here are often persecuted, as they are viewed to be competing for the same food as the grouse. The inclusion of grouse skulls in these designs was therefore an exploration of this debate, and my own reflection on whether the two could ever coexist peacefully.

Creating work in twos or threes allows me to explore each idea more thoroughly – sometimes, there is too much to learn about each subject to fit into one embroidery!

· · · · · · · · · · ·

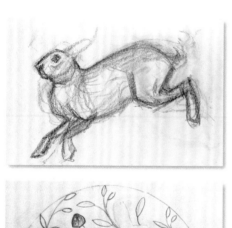

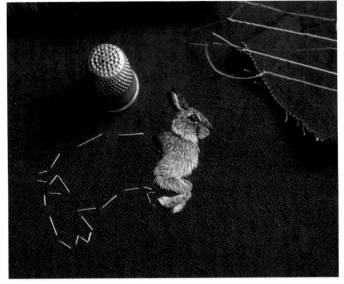

Working on a dark navy background allowed the opportunity to use brighter-coloured threads, creating a greater, more effective contrast between the two – this is why I opted for red fly agaric mushrooms, rather than a more common cream or brown variation.

• • • • • • • • • • •

As these two pieces were designed as a pair, originally I stitched both on one piece of fabric – albeit at enough distance to cut around them later. This allowed me to take care that they were in harmony with one another throughout the embroidering process. In addition, I gave both designs repeating mushroom and grouse skull motifs to suggest the story behind them and further show their connection to each other.

Ending up with the little matching pair I had envisioned and sketched weeks before was incredibly satisfying. They are simple designs, but sometimes keeping extra details to a minimum can really benefit the animals at the centre of the design.

'Hare in Flowers'

2018

Finished in a 15.25cm (6in) hoop

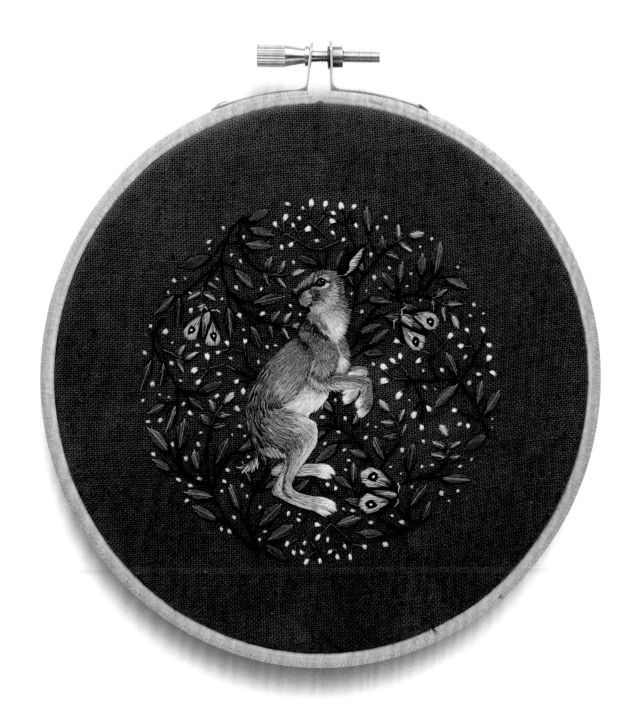

I wanted to play around with the position of the hare in this embroidery and so decided to depict him alert, on his hind legs with his head turned towards the source of his alarm. It looks fairly simple now! However, portraying the hare looking over his shoulder was actually quite tricky to achieve.

· · · · · · · · · ·

I spent some time looking at reference photos of hares in various turned poses, to see how their fur splayed out across the shoulders. I then got to work with the main drawing, which would help me navigate the piece with thread later on.

Often, especially nowadays when I am more confident in my design process, I work mostly with one sketch - erasing and redrawing it until I am happy with how it looks. Here, I wanted to be sure that the head looked like it flowed from the neck, rather than appearing stuck on.

I envisioned a very dense background for this design, as you can see above. As well as the plants and moths, I filled any gaps with little pink and white petals, which I planned to colour with pink and white threads later.

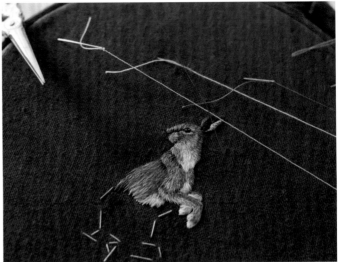

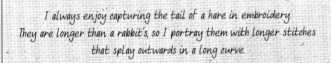

I always enjoy capturing the tail of a hare in embroidery.
They are longer than a rabbit's, so I portray them with longer stitches
that splay outwards in a long curve.

. . . .

I had a lot of fun with this piece, in addition to exploring and playing around
with the hare's position. I wanted to go with a fairly muted colour scheme
for the background fabric and flora. I used an unobtrusive navy fabric, and
then kept the leaves of the plants quite dark, with the flower buds shifting in
between white and a soft pink. This meant that, despite the detail involved in
the background, it did not draw the viewer's eye away from the hare.

The process of creating this embroidery was very smooth, both in planning and stitching, as hares by now were a subject with which I was very comfortable.

•   •   •   •   •   •   •   •   •   •

As mountain hares hold so much fascination for me, with their changeable appearance, I always love to analyze, capture and experiment with the colours found in their fur, and find new ways of representing them in thread. In this case, I had been looking at photos of mountain hares caught in the transition between early and mid-winter, halfway through growing their snowy coats. In my preliminary sketch, I took care to note the darker hairs over their heads and backs while the new white fur bloomed across their bellies, down the front of their legs and up their necks.

Adding the eye highlights always gives more character to the animal. Until this point, the stitching can look a bit flat and lifeless; the glint of light is what brings the creature to life.

In this piece, I wanted to use the moths to add little touches of gold to the composition. I often use moths in this manner, as they are a good way to add flashes of colour that would not necessarily work in the plants.

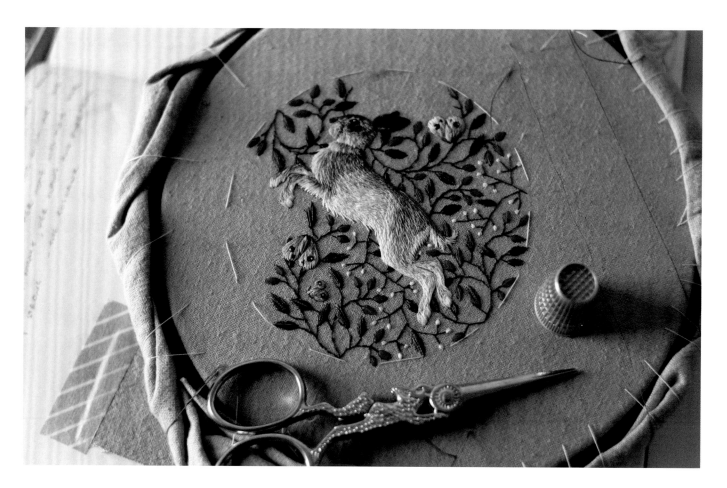

· · · · · · · · · · ·

When designing this piece, I wanted to create a background that would contain traditional Christmas colours – green, red and gold – without it becoming garish. Using a subtle blue fabric as the main 'backdrop' to the composition, I kept the greens quite subdued, only using three different tones throughout. I also tried not to overcomplicate things by filling every gap with flora, like I did in the 'Hare in Flowers' piece.

Approaching the design in this way worked well: as the colours of the leaves were knocked back (muted), they did not conflict with the fabric or the brighter threads in this piece. In addition, by adding the brighter colours as smaller accents in the moths and flora, they were not too loud and did not draw attention away from the hare itself.

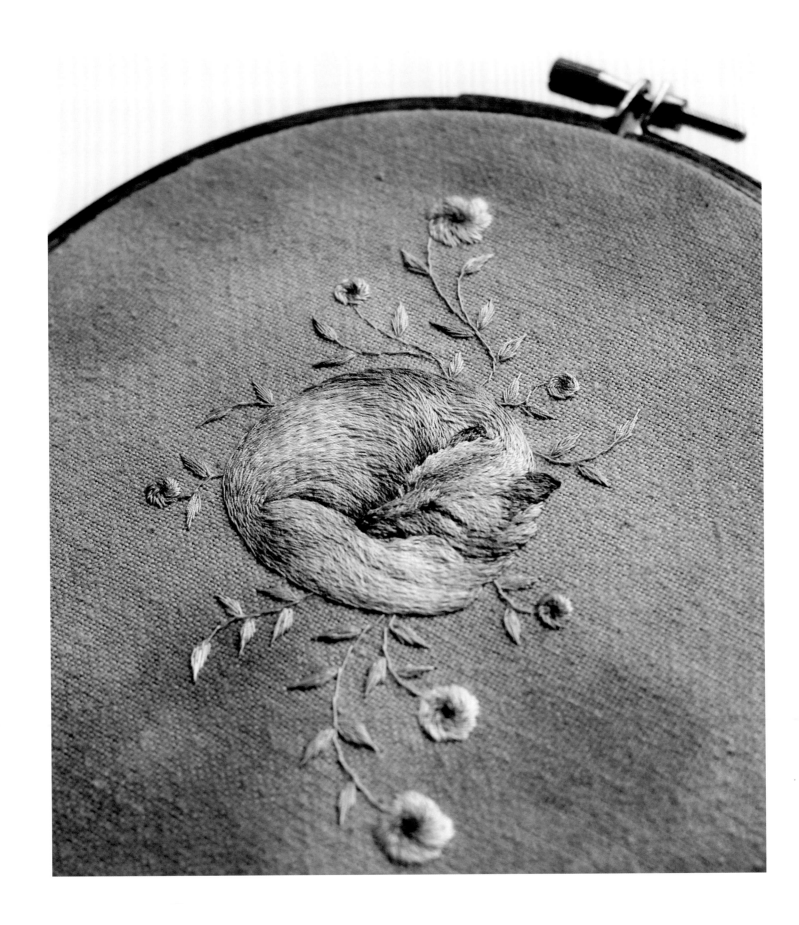

Foxes

Foxes hold a special place in our folklore – loved as mischief makers and loathed as pests. Wild and yet increasingly urban, they are a fascinating subject to explore in thread, and are probably one I will be returning to for years to come.

When I first set out to embroider foxes, one particular element I was interested in capturing was the eye-catching shifts of colour across their bodies – from black to bright orange, and the unsaturated greys that often appear over their hindquarters.

. . . .

'Dormant Fox'

2015

Finished in a 12.75cm (5in) hoop

This was one of my first pieces in what would become my needle-painting technique. A lot of my earliest animal embroideries show the subject asleep. This was partly due to me enjoying how peaceful and serene this made them look, but also because I knew showing an animal awake would be more difficult to embroider: it would require really capturing the character and expression in their faces. As I improved my technique over the years, I gained more confidence and started to wake them up.

• • • • • • • • • • •

I began by doing some drawings from several references – from photographs and illustrations in anatomy books – to get a feel for foxes and how they move, and see how their fur blends together. Once I had studied the fox's body in detail, I moved on to playing around with ideas for a final embroidery. As I was not overly familiar with foxes when I started this design, I spent some time redrawing particular features, especially the eyes, until I felt confident about how they looked.

There was a lot to consider when selecting the colours I would use. The oranges were an easy choice, but I also wanted to show the subtle greys you can see in a fox's coat that often sit along their back and hindquarters.

As this was one of my first embroideries using sewing thread rather than embroidery thread, 'Dormant Fox' was a huge learning curve in how I applied my needle-painting technique: I was learning how to manage all the changes in thread direction in a piece of a substantial size. This is when I began to realize how important the sketchbook work was in helping me navigate all the complexities of a freehand embroidery.

As this was one of my first pieces, I worked much more slowly than I would now, and I repeatedly checked photo references of foxes to make sure I was accurately depicting their coat colours.

Although I always try not to rush my work, I also find stopping and starting too much can interrupt the flow of the embroidery, and this is something I think this piece was affected by. If I was to re-create it now, I would work on it continuously for solid blocks of time, which I believe would have given the piece a greater sense of fluidity and cohesiveness.

. . . .

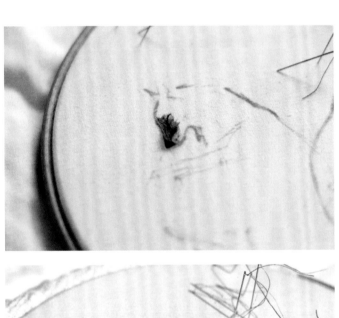

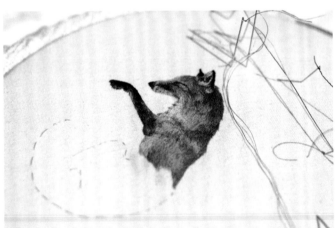
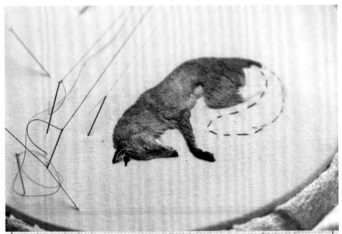

Getting a handle on colour blending was important. As well as using various tones to create the lights and darks one would see in a sleeping fox, I had to remember to add in evenly spaced stitches of grey to create a mottled effect in certain parts of the coat.

This was the biggest embroidery I had completed at the time, and I am grateful for everything it taught me for the future. I went on from this piece with a greater understanding of the needle-painting technique I was developing – how to choose and blend colours, to control the thread direction, and also to have the patience to work for longer stretches of time.

'Arctic Fox'
2016

Finished in a 15.25cm (6in) hoop

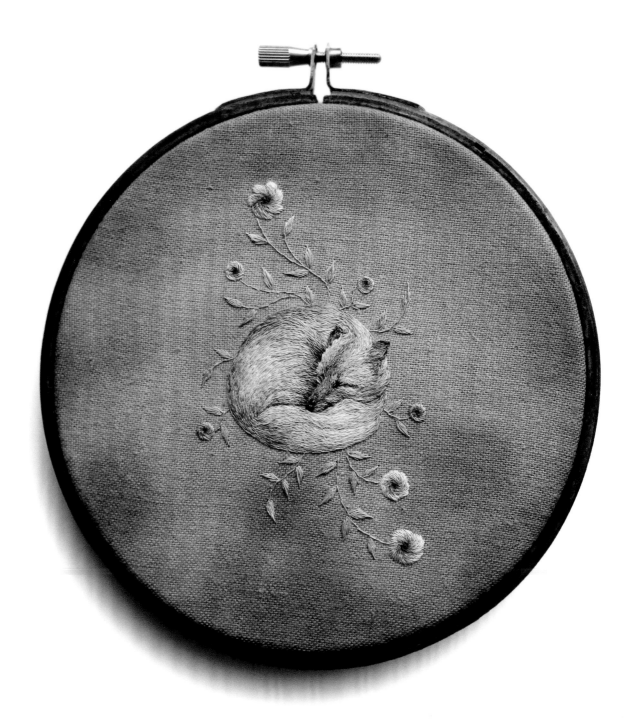

I am captivated by the luscious coats of arctic foxes.
I had them in mind as a subject for one of my embroideries,
as I wanted to capture the copious folds of fur which gather
when these foxes curl up to sleep.

. . . .

To begin, I looked at different reference photographs of arctic foxes awake
and sleeping, but I also drew inspiration from various other creatures whose
fur spread in a similar way when sleeping – red foxes, wolves and even house
cats – to get a well-rounded knowledge of how the fox's fur would behave in
this position.

Like the mountain hares, the fur of arctic foxes changes between summer and
winter, and I was interested in creating the colour shifts myself in stitch. In
the end, I gave this one a darker coat, flecked with beige and brown threads,
thus presenting a fox more reminiscent of its summer coat than the pure
white one of winter.

I began thinking of the fabric I wanted to use for this piece back when I was working on the preliminary sketches. I was inspired by images of night skies I had seen, where distant galaxies created a mottled effect in the colour of the sky. To re-create this effect on fabric, I applied concentrated amounts of dye to darken particular areas of the fabric, leaving the centre mostly untouched to create a spotlight in which the fox would eventually slumber.

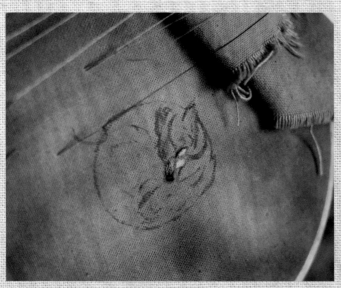

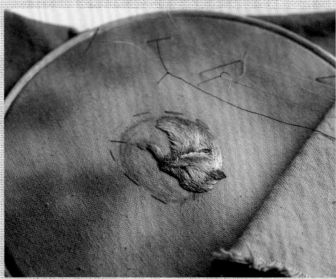

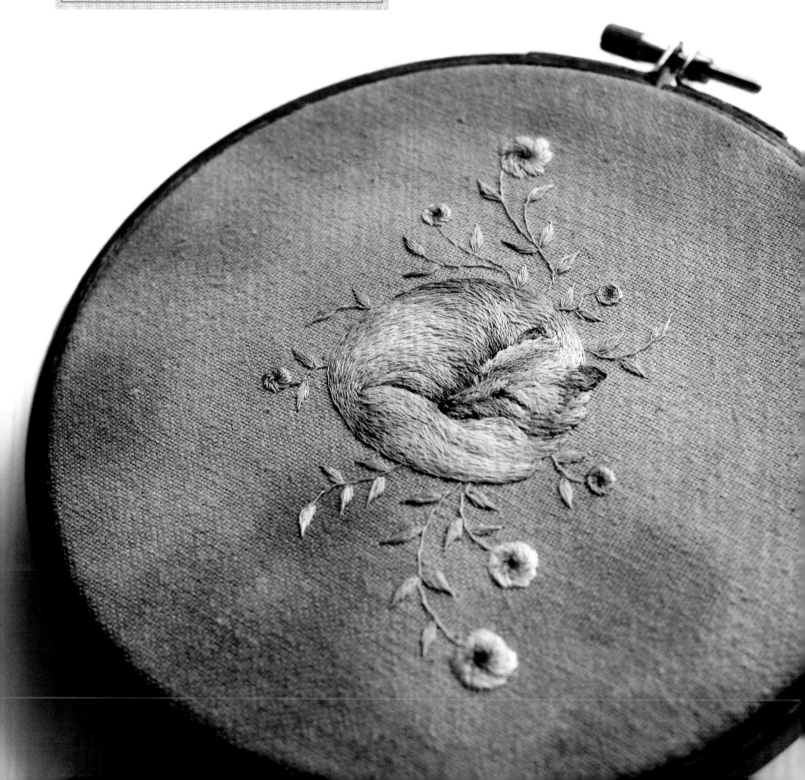

'Springing Fox'

2017

Finished in a 10cm (4in) hoop

. . . .

I had a very specific silhouette in mind prior to
preparing this design, so getting the majority of the
sketch down for the final piece proved very easy.

I had been looking at several pictures of foxes leaping in snow, and had spent time analyzing and drawing the shape of their bodies on the cusp of pouncing. The only real departure from the pictures I drew from was the decision to wrap the tail neatly around the back legs, to fit it within a circular composition.

I did end up drawing out the face a number of times until I was happy with the fox's expression. As I never have a single reference photograph to work from, I often have to redraw elements of the design until I hit on what I have in mind.

. . . .

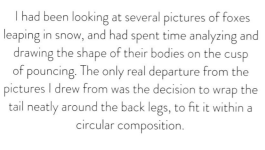

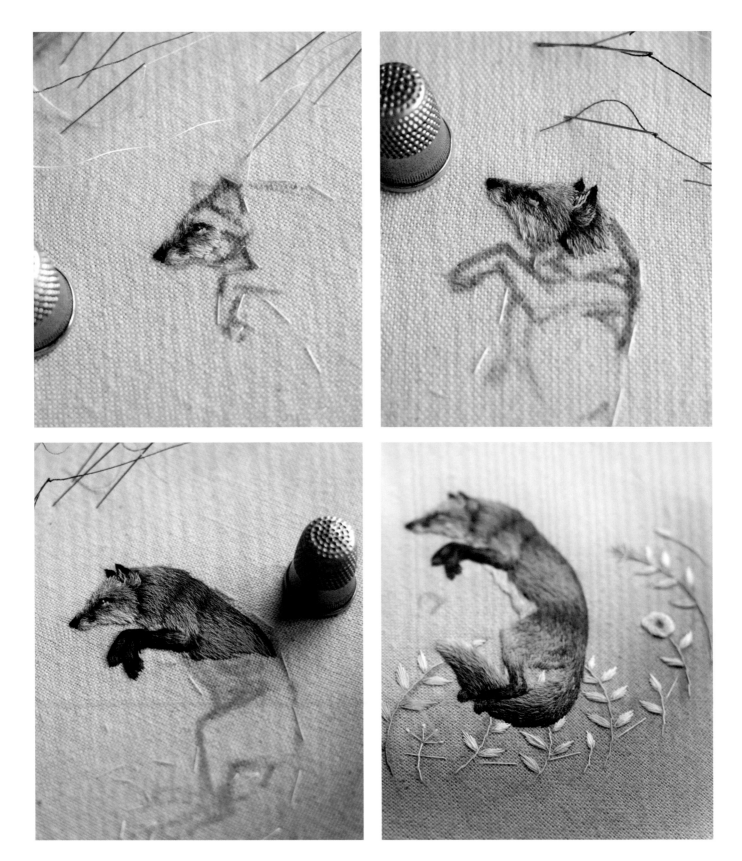

Like my earlier mountain hare embroideries, I hand-dyed the fabric with varying amounts of dye to create a gradient of colour in the background, darker at one edge and allowing the fabric naturally to form a glow just off the centre, to bring the focus of the composition towards the fox's head. I had in mind frosty mornings when I was choosing my fabric, dyes and thread colours, when early light is muted and glowing across the country landscape, and plants are covered in a layer of frost.

. . . .

I love the final effect of the fox's rich red fur on this blue fabric. I really tried to push my abilities and portray the leaping fox as accurately as I could in this piece, as it was only my second attempt at stitching foxes. Hopefully, I succeeded in creating his multi-toned coat with cohesiveness and nuance.

'Fox Kit, Standing'
2017

Finished in a 10cm (4in) hoop

· · · · · · · · · ·

After my earlier pieces, I was inspired to keep experimenting with foxes as a subject. Choosing to portray a young fox this time, known as a kit, instead of an adult meant I could work smaller, making it easier to play around with the pose of the fox.

Sketching a young fox meant I focused on keeping the body more rounded, as the lean muscles seen in an adult have not yet developed. I also enlarged features like the eyes and ears slightly, just as one would do for a human child. Once I had worked out the key points that separated a juvenile fox from an adult one, it was simple to create the final drawing from which to work.

Prior to stitching, I worked a test painting of this piece in my sketchbook, to see if the bright oranges of the fox would work on a bright blue background. Up to this point I had only embroidered foxes on undyed fabric, or on more subdued shades of blue.

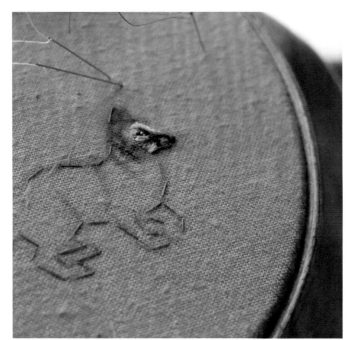

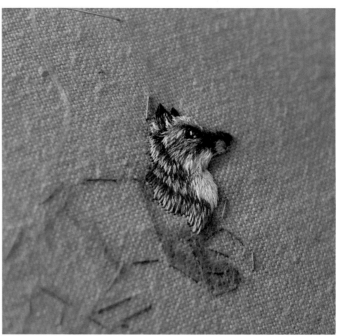

This was another design where I did not want the background detail to detract from the main subject. Therefore, I kept the flashes of red in the flowers very small, and worked the moths in a blue that echoed the blue in the background fabric, so that they added enough detail without becoming too loud.

I felt confident about stitching foxes by this point so this particular piece came together easily and quickly. I particularly enjoyed incorporating and stitching in the ruffles of fur along the neck and shoulders – a feature I had noted in reference photos of kits, owing to the lovely, fluffy coats they have at that young age.

. . . .

'Sleeping Fox Kit'

2017

Finished in a 10cm (4in) hoop

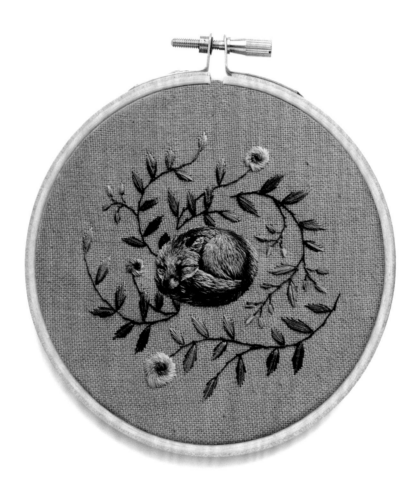

• • • • • • • • • • • •

With this piece I wanted to revisit the pose of the arctic
fox I had embroidered earlier on (see page 74), this
time with a young red fox.

cogs+s - 11.30am

blue flowers and berries?

pink water

GREENS
8812, 7223, 394, 582

BLUES
13, 112, 311, 5826, 276

PINKS
519, 79, 938,
165, 658.

I always find things I could improve upon in my work. When designing this new fox, I tried to incorporate everything I felt worked in the 'Arctic Fox' piece, and to approach the parts I did not think worked well before in a new way. Here, in particular, I wanted to work on the face of the fox – how I could give the closed eyes a more realistic appearance.

As I really wanted the colours to pop in this piece, I selected the most vibrant oranges for the fox and settled on a baby pink for the flower buds, to contrast deliberately with the blue background. Before committing anything to thread, I made a quick gouache painting in my sketchbook, to see if these colours would work together.

. . . .

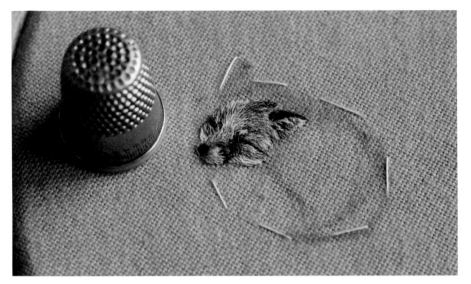

Curled-up animals always present a challenge when it comes to stitching the fur. In this situation, I make sure to keep referring back to my drawing whenever I need a stronger idea of where and how my stitches should lie. It is by using these final drawings that I have 'problem solved' most of the complicated parts of a creature's body – from what sections of fur should run together through to working out exactly where light and dark tones are to go. Sticking to the original drawing for these more troublesome sections also means I do not have to worry about keeping everything in proportion as I work.

This being a younger fox meant I needed to ensure I had exaggerated the size of the head and eyes, as this is usually the easiest way to portray a youthful character.

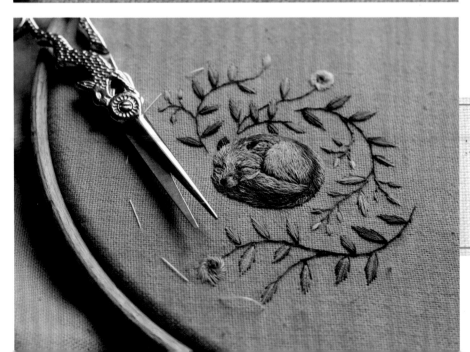

I always enjoy using these baby-pink threads for the surrounding flora on a blue background. The contrast between the two makes the buds seem to pop up from the fabric.

Although I was happy with how I handled the face of this little fox, I think my favourite part was where I was able to work really deep oranges and reds into the stripe over the hindquarters that then became his bushy tail. These vivid touches are so important in creating a three-dimensional appearance.

Fawns

Many of my embroideries are of fawns. I think they hold a special place in our imaginations, being fragile and childlike as they are, yet wild and unfamiliar too.

I have always been enraptured by their coats, which form a beautiful transition from deep, rich browns to gold and cream, interspersed with delicate spots. It is this feature that proves most challenging to embroider, but it is a challenge I will forever look forward to.

. . . .

'Fawn'
2014

Finished in a 15.25cm (6in) hoop

This sleeping fawn was one of my earliest
embroideries, and it has proven to be one of my
most popular designs.

• • • • • • • • • •

I was not anywhere near as confident with how to portray fawns as I am now.
I also had not honed my initial sketching process as I have now: I did not
explore and research the subject in my sketchbook prior to starting as I know
now I should have. This made things a bit difficult later on, as it meant I had
to make a lot of decisions on the fly! How do I redirect the threads to form
the ear? How do I create the darkest patches where the fawn's neck is leaning
over its body? These are things I now take care to think through before
I embroider, and then sketch in detail in my final drawings.

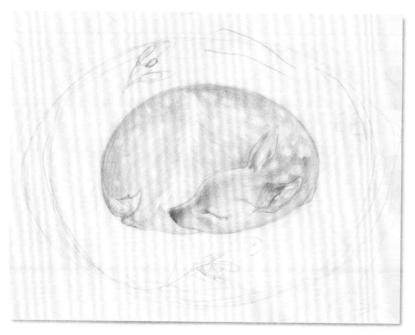

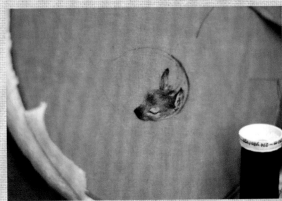

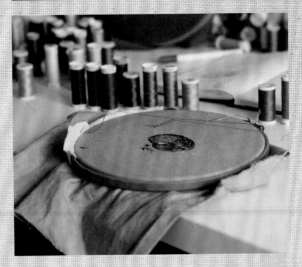

In my earlier pieces, like this one, I had not yet developed my 'love' of incredibly detailed backdrops for my animals. Instead, I liked to opt for a simple ring of plants – here, purple speedwell, cornflowers and poppies, along with some rich greens for the stems and leaves.

I chose these plants mostly for experimental reasons, to try out colours I had been keen to explore and stitch with.

I was happy with my progress on this piece until I hit the ears and lower section of the neck – I felt I had stitched the neck too wide and hadn't defined the ears enough. I was so convinced that the embroidery was ruined that I nearly threw it away and started again!

At the last minute, I decided to stick with it as I had already poured hours into working on it (I worked a lot more slowly back then), and I am so glad I did. As I added more of the fawn's body, the neck balanced out and the dark tones in the fur around the ears added the much-needed definition I had felt I was lacking.

I rarely restart pieces now, as I have come to realize that most of my embroideries go through this stage: early in the design, there is a moment when the embroidery looks as though it is going in the wrong direction. Through time and experience, I have learned to trust my ability, and know that the design will come together eventually.

. . . .

'Standing Fawn'

2017

Finished in a 12.75cm (5in) hoop

This embroidery was the first time I had revisited the subject of fawns since I created 'Fawn' back in 2014, so I was a bit nervous about doing a good job of it.

• • • • • • • • • • • •

I spent longer at the sketchbook stage than I had done before. I began by doing some loose sketches to warm up, followed by some more detailed studies from reference photographs of fawns – especially of their heads – so I could learn as much as possible about their features and expressions. I then redrew and refined the final drawing several times until I was completely happy with it. I was very focused on capturing the deep brown tone over the fawn's shoulder and hindquarters, which would really pop on the baby pink background fabric.

The fabric was also another step into an untrodden path for me; up to this point, pink was a colour I had not really used for backgrounds.

• • • • • • • • • • •

I knew from the beginning that I wanted the flowers in this design to be blue, as I knew the hue would complement the pink background perfectly (based on how well pink flowers had sat on the blue in my previous designs, and the gouache tests I made above). However, I did mix some light pink and soft lilac threads in the flowers at the bottom of the piece, to help soften the transition.

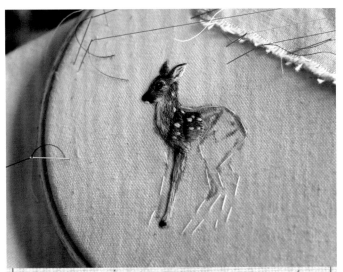

If you look closely, you might notice that I did not follow my
original drawing completely. When it comes to adding certain
details, like the spots in the fawn's coat, I often prefer to make
decisions on how to stitch them as I go along. Features like these
are small enough that artistic licence can be used. Furthermore,
not worrying about following the sketch absolutely means
I am better able to see what would work best with the flow
of stitches while embroidering.

I definitely fell in love with the pink fabric, and have used variations of it many times since. The addition of blue flowers, and the touch of blue dye at the bottom edge to harmonize the two colours further, really set off the pink.

I had been most concerned about being able to catch a sense of character and life in the fawn's expression, but my earlier studies based on the several references I had gathered gave me the knowledge (and the confidence) I needed to work these elements into the stitches. As this was quite a simple pose to work with, I was looking forward to trying something more complex next time!

. . . .

Despite my initial nervousness, this piece was a dream to stitch! The extra work I had put in early on in the sketchbook was worth it, as I felt confident about what tones should go where and how to handle all the colour shifts across the body of the fawn.

**When it came to designing this particular embroidery,
I wanted to create a more vivacious fawn than I had previously
embroidered: usually, my pieces capture animals while they
are slumbering.**

· · · · · · · · · ·

As is often the case, I had a particular composition in mind before starting the piece.
I deliberately sought out a suitable reference that matched the idea I had in my head, and
analyzed the parts of the deer I was most interested in – particularly how deer hold their
forelegs and head in such a pose. Originally, I had the fawn's head angled slightly towards
the viewer, but in time decided to change this so that the head was completely in profile,
to create a stronger silhouette. It was then, after making these adjustments, that I drew the
final image of the fawn from my imagination.

When it came to choosing the colours for this fawn, I wanted to see how the spots in the
coat would show on lighter-coloured fur – how they would fade in and out of view as the
coat changed colour. I had worked with similar colour palettes when stitching mountain
hares, so I was looking forward to returning to this range of threads once again.

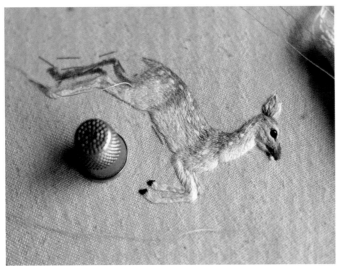 

• • • • • • • • • •

Portraying a white or cream animal is always a bit tricky.

As I had done in the past with 'Winter Blue Hare' (see page 51), before I began I picked out a beige thread to be my darkest tone, the only exception being the muzzle which naturally has a very dark colour. Choosing this darkest thread early on is important for this reason; otherwise, it is tempting to keep adding deeper browns or greys right to up the colour contrast (such as the change from the snowy shade of colour at the front that gradually shifts to a silvery-brown colour towards the back of the neck). Picking too dark a thread can give a muddy appearance to the fur.

The choice of fabric played an important part too. The soft pink of the background fabric helped lessen the effect of the deeper browns, bringing out the warmer tones in the deer's coat.

Originally, I intended to have a detailed background for this piece, made up mostly of simple leaves. However, when I began filling in the design, I realized that the dark green leaves would be too heavy and distracting next to the light-coloured fawn.

I unpicked all the flora and started again, this time working only two plants at the bottom of the hoop that I then finished off with light-coloured flowers. This less imposing background gave the fawn room to breathe in the composition. Situations like these are a good example of why wholly adhering to a preliminary sketch can be unnecessary; had I continued, the design would have been too busy and not as impactful.

. . . .

This is the only white fawn I have ever embroidered. If I ever return to the subject it would be interesting to try out a darker background, to see how the whites and creams would glow on deeper colours.

'Fawn Below a Bower'
2018

Finished in a 15.25cm (6in) hoop

This piece very much resembles my earlier embroidery of a standing fawn, but this time explores a slightly different stance and features a variation on my usual flora – an overhanging tree branch. When I become interested in a subject, I love returning to it again and again to find new ways of rendering it in stitch.

. . . .

While sketching, I played around with the shape of the fawn's head and paid extra attention to the eyes and the bones that underlie the facial structure, as these were areas I was looking to try to improve upon in this piece.

Most of the time, I design the foliage for my animals so it either entirely encircles the animal or rises up from the bottom of the hoop, which I feel adds a bit of energy and movement to the composition. This time, I decided to add overhanging branches instead; these give a sense of protection and coziness to the scene.

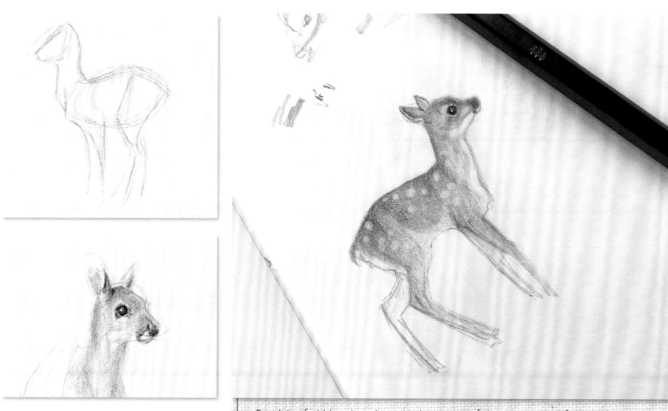

Do not be afraid to return to a subject once again if it inspires you, as there is a lot you can continue to discover – you can never manage to explore everything in a single embroidery. Here, I moved the position of the fawn's legs a little, just to experiment with having the fawn seem more alert this time.

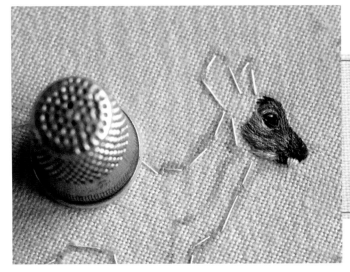

Stitching the fawn's face was probably my favourite part of this embroidery. I could never get bored of attempting to capture all the folds of fur around a fawn's eye, and endeavouring to add some of the character of the real creature.

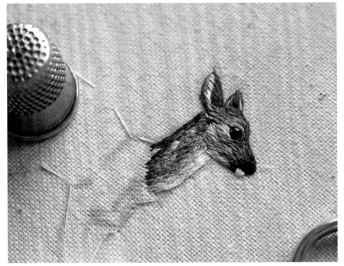

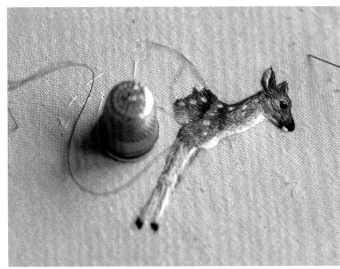

When stitching fawns, I find it necessary to keep referring back to my drawing to meld the shifting tones of the coat with the spots sprinkled over the top, just so that I do not get too caught up in one or the other. For this particular fawn, which has a more unusual pose, I looked to my final drawing more scrupulously than I usually would.

To suggest the more alert stance of the fawn, I gave it a small tilt to the back legs; in addition, the ears were angled back and the eyes made slightly wider. Despite this tension in the fawn, the falling flowers and surrounding branches still bring a sense of calm to the composition.

. . . .

'Winter Fawn'

2018

Finished in a 15.25cm (6in) hoop

With this embroidery, I returned to a pose I love for my creatures – curled up and nestled down to sleep – but this time with the hope of catching a bit of festive spirit.

• • • • • • • • • •

The first challenge with this piece was to convey the season inspiring the piece through the background details, but without those same features taking the focus away from the animal at the centre of the composition.

The preliminary sketch I eventually worked from also required more time and effort than usual, and it was redrawn several times until I felt satisfied with it. In the past, I had struggled to keep everything looking 'three-dimensional' when designing an animal in this pose; so, for this design, I went over my sketch again and again. I reworked the folds in the fawn's shoulder and hindquarters, until I was confident that working from this drawing would give me the final embroidery I wanted.

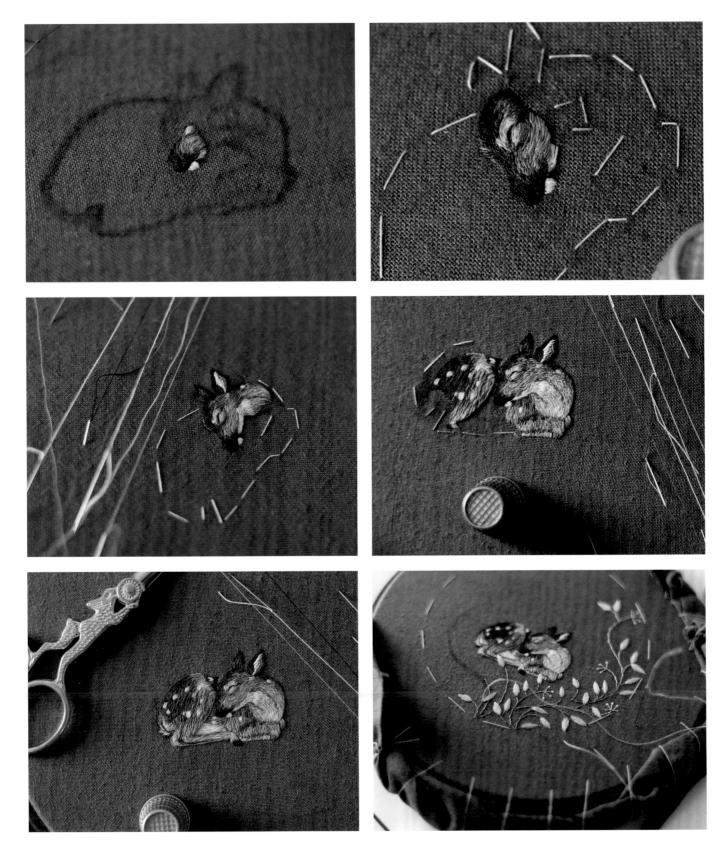

• • • • • • • • • •

First wash of
blue dye...

It took me a couple of attempts to dye the background fabric to this deep royal blue successfully. Although it is tempting to add black to the mix to achieve a darker colour, doing so would give the fabric a dull, grey appearance.

Instead, I have found that the best way to create richer blues is to stick to ones that have purple tones; I then steadily add these one wash at a time until I am left with a deeper colour. Sometimes, I will even add a touch of pure purple dye to the dyed-blue fabric: this is not enough to turn the fabric purple, but rather adds a depth and vibrancy to the blue. This background colour also works well in bringing out the lovely reds and golds in the robins and fawn.

... second wash of
blue dye.

• • • • • • • • • •

I had wanted to create a fawn embroidery in this winter setting for quite a while, so finally making it happen was satisfying. When working several elements together in one embroidery, I find it helpful to limit the colour palette to keep everything cohesive. In this case, keeping the plants blue to correspond with the background, and using the same browns for the robins as I did for the fawn, pulled the composition together and added balance. Furthermore, the strongest seasonal elements in the piece - the red breasts of the robins - could then stand out against everything else.

Rabbits

Out of all the creatures I stitch and draw, rabbits are easily the ones I am most comfortable with rendering on fabric. Compared to the other animals, I rely a lot less on references for them, and draw most of my initial rabbit designs straight from my imagination.

Rabbits are often associated with rebirth and new life in folklore, and I think that is what draws me to them so often. They make for vibrant, familiar little subjects, and there is always something new to explore when embroidering them, whether it be the endless variations in their coats or the challenge of capturing their playful nature.

· · · · · · · · · ·

'Baby Rabbits'

2016–2017

Finished in a 7.6cm (3in) hoop

I envisioned these two little rabbits as a duo, echoing their main background motifs – the moths and mushrooms – across each piece to bring them together. However, I was keen to keep the colours and poses slightly different to make them individual pieces in their own right too.

. . . .

I wanted to work as small as possible for these baby rabbits (even by my own standards!), in order to try to portray their delicacy and character.

The rabbit on the left was the first of the two I worked on. I made a lot of quick, loose sketches before picking a selection of the strongest drawings to develop and work up the final reference illustration. Ideally, I wanted to end up with drawings that, although detailed, still had a sense of movement and energy to them.

Once I began the second rabbit of the pair, on the right, I was in the swing of things and had the look of the baby rabbits, and their composition, completed.

I designed the surrounding flora for the rabbits so that they were a bit smaller than I normally would have them, to harmonize with the size of the rabbits. I did not want them drowned out by large leaves!

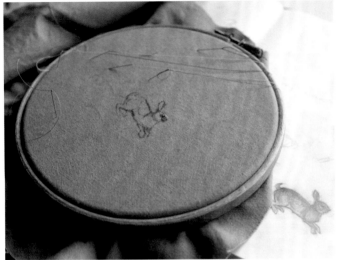

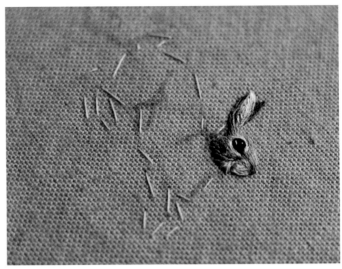

To keep things interesting, for these little rabbits I experimented with how I captured the eye, making it a bit larger and more prominent than I would usually. Adding in the moths and the mushrooms on such a small composition was worth the bother: on the blue background, they look like little jewels.

· · · · · · · · · ·

I have stitched so many rabbits that they have become a very familiar subject to me. However, whenever I work on a design with one as the subject, I still enjoy looking for elements I could do differently from the last time, whether it be how I portray the colour and texture of the fur, or the expression in the rabbit's face.

Working so small did add an extra challenge to these rabbits, as you have fewer stitches to get the overall design across, but ultimately they became fun little embroideries to do.

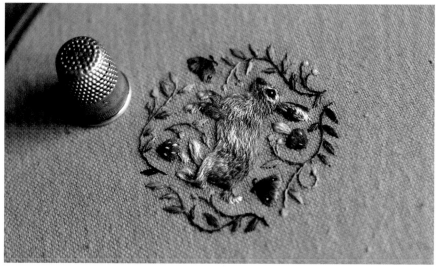

'Sleeping Rabbit'

2017

Finished in a 7.6cm (3in) hoop

· · · · S l e e p i n g · R a b b i t · · · ·

A lot of people find my sleeping animals a touch too mournful, but my feelings are quite the opposite: I am always fascinated by the sense of peace and calm that can be found in restful images.

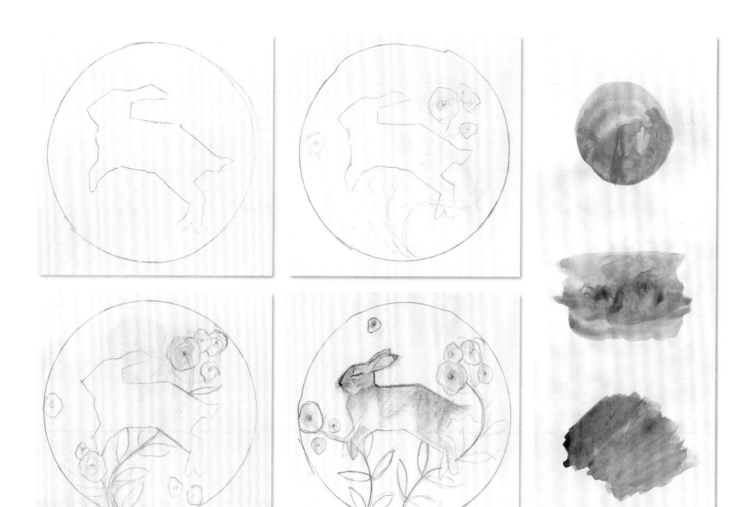

I kept the design quite simple for this piece. I wanted to experiment with various colours for the flowers and fabric background, so I needed to take care that the overall embroidery would not become too busy.

Like my earliest fox embroidery (see page 70), this rabbit is lying down on its side. To some this can make the animal seem lifeless, but I find myself drawn to compositions like this: there is a peacefulness I see in the animal in this state, and a graceful arrangement in their limbs.

I used gouache paints to try out a few ideas for background colours in my sketchbook before dyeing the fabric. Blending blues and pinks always makes me think of beautiful early morning skies.

· · · · · · · · · · ·

If you look closely at the rabbit's ear, you can see a suggestion of pastel pink – this is the same colour thread used for the flowers. Keeping to a limited colour palette can encourage a more cohesive, balanced design.

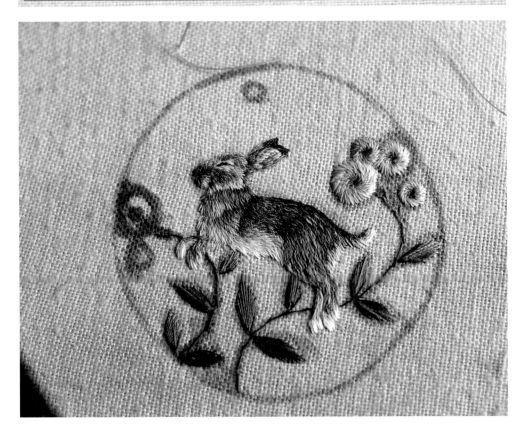

. . . .

My intention with a piece this petite was always to frame it within a smaller hoop, such as a 7.6cm (3in) hoop, so that the little design would not get lost in too much fabric.

When stitching the flowers, I finished each of the 'background' flowers by edging them with a light blue. This was so their shapes could meld gently into the fabric, and not break the soft appearance of the overall embroidery. In addition, tinging these background buds with blue meant the rabbit and the two foreground flowers could be brought forward, further suggesting the focal point of the picture: the sleeping rabbit.

I loved working on this multicoloured fabric. It allowed me to mimic the colour shifts used in parts of the embroidery, such as the flowers, and make the fabric feel as much a part of the composition as the main embroidery itself. This is a technique I have continued to use in other pieces, to carry the mood of the embroidery across the entire work.

'Rabbits on Navy'
2017

Finished in 10cm (4in) hoops

· · · · · · · · · ·

With this trio I wanted to revisit the aesthetic of my earlier
'Sleeping Rabbit' piece, not only with the rabbit's pose but also
the background flowers – I often either fill the entire background
with plants, or have them only at the bottom of the design;
here, I wanted to do something different.

I wanted to play around with having only a small bunch of flowers behind each rabbit, leaving the rest of the background as a negative space. This simplicity makes the pink of the flowers on the dark blue fabric much more striking.

As I was working on a darker background, I decided to push the contrasts in the rabbit's fur a bit more, incorporating more dark browns and greys as they worked nicely with the deep navy fabric.

Compared to hares, rabbits have less muscle definition and shorter limbs, so I worked on these areas carefully to ensure this distinction was acknowledged. I also added more fur, fluffing out at the edges of their bodies, to describe their rounder forms.

Creating these rabbits in a set of three was an opportunity to spend some time experimenting with all these different factors. It is also fun to have each piece play off the others when doing sets like this – in this case, having the two active rabbits leaping away from the sleeping one in the centre.

. . . .

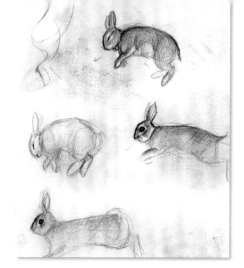

'Watchful Rabbit'

2017

Finished in a 10cm (4in) hoop

• • • • • • • • • •

One of the reasons my animals are nearly always asleep or in motion is that it can be very hard to stop a design looking stiff when the animal is only standing, as in this piece.

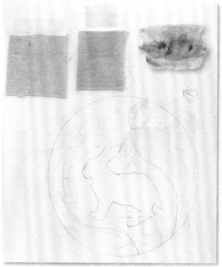

· · · · · · · · · · ·

I spent a great deal of time drawing the rabbit for this design in my sketchbook,
trying to keep this rabbit looking lively and fluid despite it being stationary.
In addition, I focused hard on capturing the qualities of an apprehensive rabbit,
based on my reference photographs, giving him a guarded expression and having
his back legs in a crouch ready to run.

Inspired by how effective a pink background could be for my embroideries,
I decided to design and dye the pink fabric I had to add further interest and
movement to the piece. I painted a few colour tests with gouache initially; I then
cut out little squares of fabric to test the dyes properly, and see which colours
worked best on the fabric. As you can see above, I looked at several subtle
colours that I thought would work well with the pink – yellows, blues and purples.

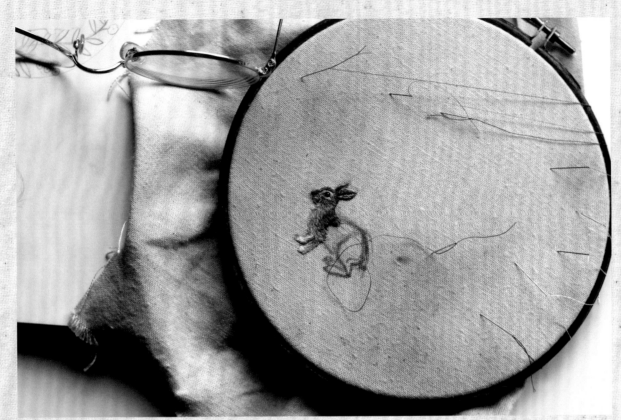

· · · · · · · · · · ·

The resulting background fabric in this case was an effective blend of pinks and purples; I also sprinkled on small grains of pure dye towards the end of the dyeing process, as the fabric was drying, which left small dots of bright pink and blue. I liked the effect on the fabric, but a lot of people thought I had actually left spots of fabric marker on the fabric – so some details are not for everyone!

Once again, I added moths to the design, using the same blues as in the flowers for their wings to balance the piece. I always like to think of moths fluttering through the undergrowth as the sun goes down, and the ethereal effect of the hand-dyed fabric for this embroidery I hope suggests this idea even more.

I had intended to have this rabbit completely surrounded and covered over by shrubbery, but as I began to stitch it seemed too overbearing. So, I cut back to just the two stems. I plan all my embroideries carefully, but sometimes it is important to not be afraid to chop and change things if they are not working.

'Standing Rabbit'

2017

Finished in a 12.75cm (5in) hoop

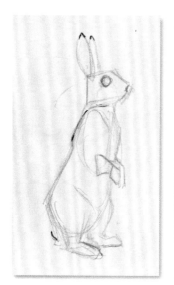

Having not embroidered a standing rabbit since an older, 2014, piece (see overleaf), I was keen to reinterpret the idea.

• • • • • • • • • •

I made several loose sketches to work out how exactly I wanted the rabbit to be posed. Although this composition was a diversion from my usual habit of drawing rabbits either running or jumping, I found these drawings fun to work with. The shape of the standing rabbit itself was quite simple, so I had only to work out details like the arrangement of the forelegs.

While in my sketchbook, I played around with ideas for the colour of my main fabric. I wanted to be able to control the colours in them much more, just as I do with thread, and decided the way to do this was to incorporate little patches of different-coloured dyes. After a couple of quick gouache tests, I dyed the background for this piece using a combination of blues, pinks and purples, keeping the fabric wet as I added each colour so that they blended into each other smoothly.

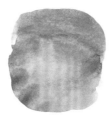

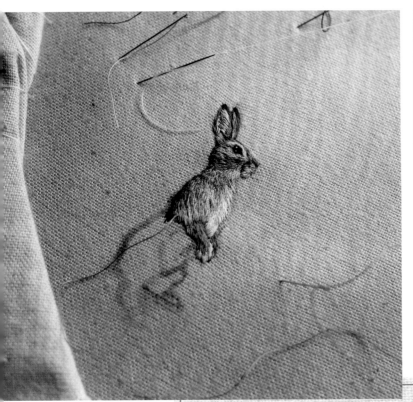

One of my favourite things about stitching the rabbit in this position was the opportunity to give more focus to the fluffy fur on the neck and stomach – parts that are often missed out when the subject is in complete profile. Small touches, like the little white stomach and scruff of fur, definitely help to give the rabbit more of the character I strive to work into my embroideries.

'Rabbit in Flowers', 2014. Finished in a 12.75cm (5in) hoop

My first standing rabbit (and, in fact, my first ever rabbit embroidery) was also my first foray into stitching flowers. The technique I used back then has remained very much the same, only I now vary the colours found within them more, often having the flowers shift and blend in with each other and the colour of the background to create a more subtle effect.

. . . .

Working the rabbit's browns and golds on to this colourful background was
wonderful. I was worried that a busy backdrop of dyed colour would detract
from the main subject, but in the end the colours all worked together
beautifully to create a soft, cohesive image.

Most of the time, I have found no amount of sketchbook work can prepare
you fully for the final embroidery; I just have to find out if my ideas are going
to work as I stitch!

🌿 *'Two Rabbits'* 🌿

2017

Finished in a 12.75cm (5in) hoop

  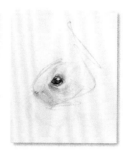

I tend to feature only one animal at a time in my embroideries,
so this design was an experiment in whether or not I could have
two similar animals in the same piece – tiny ones too! – and
have them interacting with each other.

• • • • • • • • • •

As well as continuing my own experiments and studies with fabric dye, testing different
gradients of colour with my gouache paints and playing with myriad combinations of dyes,
I was also looking at works of art to inspire palettes I had not considered before. For this
piece, I looked at paintings like J. M. W. Turner's 'The Evening Star' (c. 1830). It depicts a
sunset beach, of which almost three quarters is occupied by an atmospheric evening sky
filled with a stunning range of colours. Inspired, I added the subtle white glow of a star in the
background of 'Two Rabbits', above the rabbit on the left, just as in the painting.

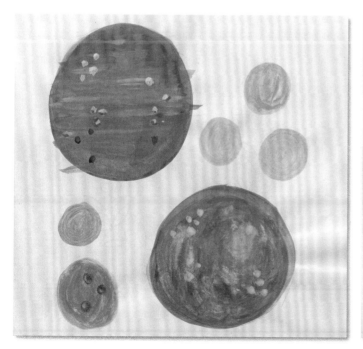 

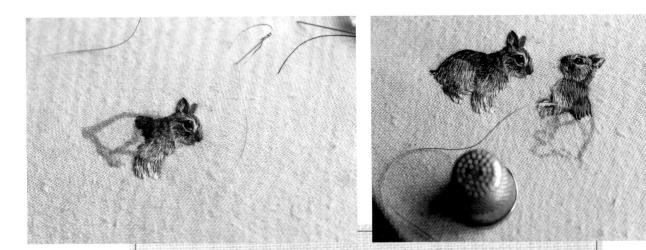

These baby rabbits were much smaller than my usual rabbit embroideries, and it was important that they came across as rabbit kits to the viewer. To convey their young age, I endeavoured to 'round' their features more, keeping their ears short and their eyes large and wide.

· · · · · · · · · · ·

I really wanted to capture a sense of an early morning sky and stillness with this embroidery, showing a pause in the play of two young rabbits. Leaving the undergrowth fairly sparse helped to achieve this, with just a few light-coloured floating flowers to bring the composition together.

Including more than one animal was a bit tricky, as I had to make sure the two figures related and played off each other; however, it is a composition I would definitely be inspired to try again.

'White Rabbit'

2017

Finished in a 15.25cm (6in) hoop

Although I had always loved the idea of stitching an animal on to black fabric, I knew I would have to consider what would work best with it. I felt a white rabbit would be a good fit, as any darker browns or greys that I would normally use for shading would fade into the dark background.

· · · · · · · · · · ·

Although I often paint little colour swatches to try out ideas for plants, I do not normally need a complete colour reference to work from and often tend to make up the rest as I go along. In this instance though, I wanted to have a rainbow effect in the flowers, the colours changing as the plants travelled around the design. I knew that without a full colour guide I would find it challenging to get all the colour transitions exactly where I wanted them once I finally started to embroider. So, I quickly put together a mock up of my intended scheme in Adobe® Photoshop® software to follow throughout the stitching process.

I love how embroideries look on black fabric but it does present additional challenges. My usual fabric pen did not show up on such a dark colour, so I had to use a chalk pencil instead – this is more challenging to work with, as it is easy to smudge the chalked outline as you work. The other issue is that black fabric is trickier to photograph! It took a lot of attempts and fiddling about with my camera settings until I was happy with the outcome.

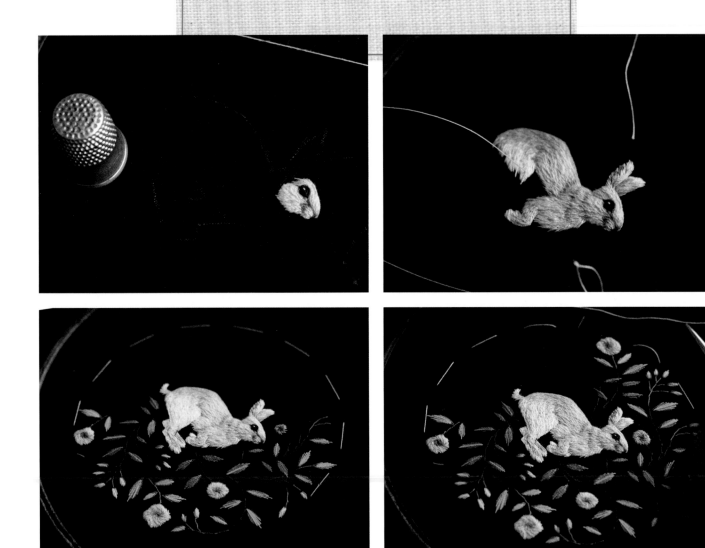

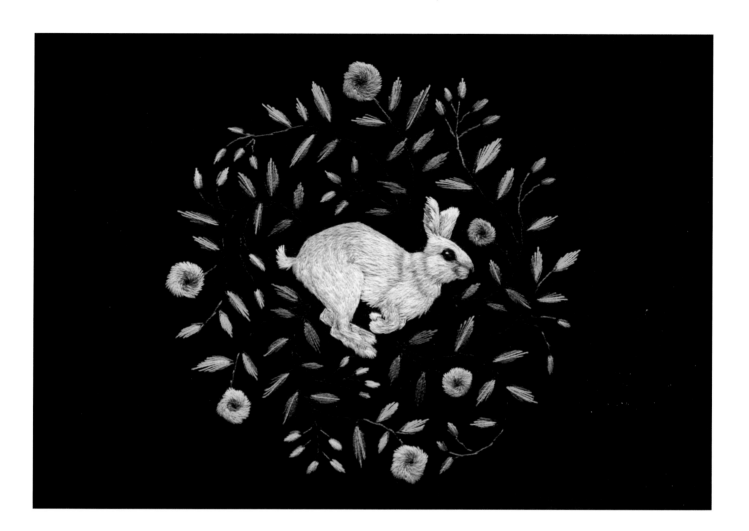

· · · · · · · · · ·

I was inspired to design this piece after doing two smaller embroideries of animal skulls on black (see page 168); this earlier experience, and using a similar colour palette too, made this rabbit easier to pull together.

I knew the colours making up the foliage would show up beautifully on the black fabric, so I incorporated lots of plants in this design to fill up all areas of the layout that would appear in the hoop (albeit leaving a nice, negative space of fabric on the outer circumference).

I normally use green threads with a yellow hue, but I have found that greens that are slightly cooler in shade, and have more of a turquoise appearance, are much more striking on black fabric.

Deeper into the Forest

I am definitely prone to going back to the same subjects again and again, but I do try to push myself to experiment with new ideas!

Although it is tempting to focus just on bigger animals, there is another world of wildlife on a smaller scale to explore. These creatures often get relegated to background details in my larger embroideries, but sometimes I get the chance to make them the main focus. For someone who already works on a small scale, these embroideries turn out to be especially minute!

Another way that I challenge myself is to work on animals I have not attempted before, such as the pine marten, the wolf and the badger cub. Exploring the new enables me to extend my knowledge of animals and further my techniques.

❦ 'Kingfisher' ❦

2015

Finished within a frame, in a 5cm (2in) square.

· · · · · · · · · · ·

I created this piece for Penguin Books to help promote their Little Black Classics series. From the hundred titles they planned, I selected a collection of poems by Gerard Manley Hopkins, which included 'As Kingfishers Catch Fire'. Capturing the feathers – especially the longer ones in the wings – is very different from portraying fur, so this piece was a bit of a challenge!

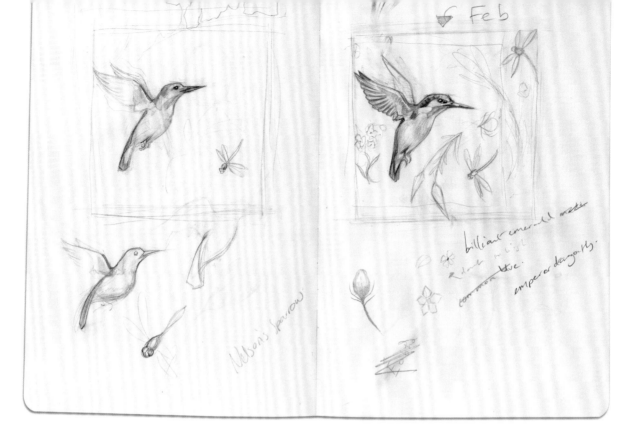

. . . .

I began by doing lots of quick sketches using lots of reference photographs, to try to get a handle on the basic shape of the kingfisher. I also worked several sketches of the smaller design elements, such as the dragonflies, to familiarize myself with their shapes as much as possible.

Once I was confident with how the bird would be posed, I moved on to a final drawing, where I then added in the finer details and a bit of tone.

In my earlier pieces, like this one, I did not draw out the backgrounds completely, and often made most of it up as I stitched. As I continued to develop my embroidery style over time, I realized that planning the whole composition allowed for a much more balanced and detailed final piece (although even now I will still adapt the design as I stitch, if I feel it is needed).

Although my work has progressed a lot since I completed this piece, I am still happy with a number of elements in it; in particular I am pleased with the dark under-feathers in the wing, as it was an area I was slightly afraid of tackling!

'Harvest Mice'

2016

Finished in 7.6cm (3in) hoops

I designed these three mice as a little trio. This was partly out of a desire to experiment with stitching increasingly tiny subjects, but also because I wanted to make collections of work and offer a more affordable option for people who wanted to own an original piece.

I had a few particular poses in mind for these mice. I always try to come up with clear and defined silhouettes before adding any detail, as this will make the final design more eye-catching for the viewer.

I also took extra care when designing the foliage for these embroideries. As the mice were so small, too much interest in the background would have easily drowned them out. I made sure no flora went over or even close to the heads of the mice, and also I tried not to go overboard with the quantity of plants included.

• • • • • • • • • •

micromys minitus

hallali

1. Resize new rabbit
2. Buy hoops - 3" + 4"
   check P+S prices
3. Photograph hares x 2
   - edit circle

psychopomp

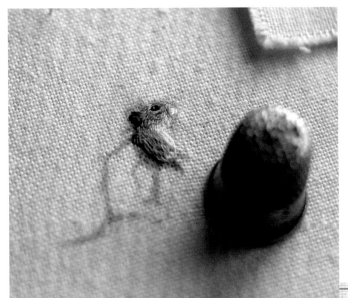

With a smaller embroidery, I try to restrict my colour palette more than usual: there is not a great deal of space for lots of colour gradations, and trying to squeeze too many in can result in the animal looking muddy and ill-defined.

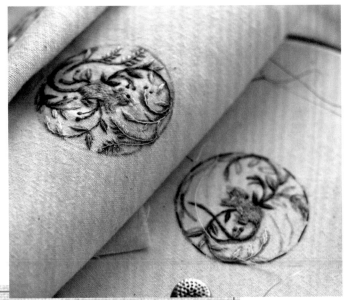

I kept these mice on undyed calico because I knew it would go well with the reds and golds of the embroidery. I originally intended for some of the plants to be green but found the colour disrupted the gentle matching tones of everything else, so I switched to gold and beige.

These little embroideries were a lesson in simplicity: working within such a small
area, and with fewer colours, every stitch has to be carefully considered –
there is no room for random stitching just to fill the space!

. . . .

ꞌHarvest Mouseꞌ

2017

Finished in a 7.6cm (3in) hoop

• • • • • • • • • • •

I revisited the harvest mice soon after the first trio, this time using a blue fabric to work on. The mouse above is one of three that I went on to sew on blue fabric.

Although the undyed calico worked well with the warm threads in the mice and flora, I find embroideries where I have selected a restricted colour palette often suit a brightly coloured background. This is a good way to add more colour without overloading the design.

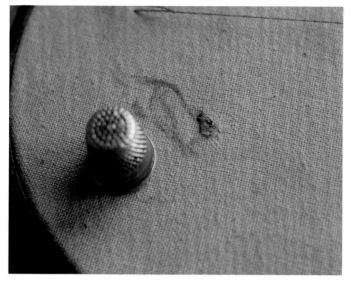

One reason I particularly enjoy embroidering harvest mice is that, unlike the wood or house mouse, their coats contain a lovely range of golds. When you have a limited range of stitches, it is nice to have more vivid colours that will catch the eye and add definition to the animal.

'Grey Squirrels'

2017

Finished in a 10cm (4in) hoop

• • • • • • • • • • •

At the time of this embroidery, I was swept up in autumnal themes and looking to create designs inspired by this season. I thought of animals beginning to build up nests for the colder months to come and, of course, squirrels came to mind.

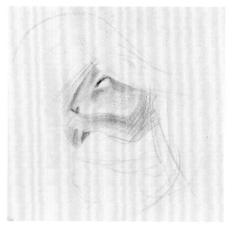

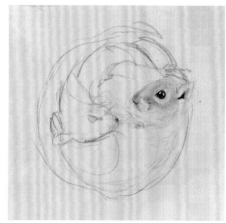

The sketch stage was especially important for this embroidery. Keeping the squirrels intertwined meant I had to consider the directions of the thread even more carefully than usual, following the natural contours of their bodies. I did not want the fur of each squirrel to blend into the other.

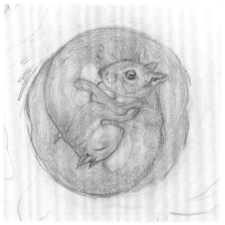

Another factor that was essential to this piece was the choice of colours. I tried to arrange the composition so that opposing colours were next to each other as much as possible – such as the light underbelly of one squirrel being placed against the dark grey of the other's head. This stopped this piece turning into a puddle of greys and browns!

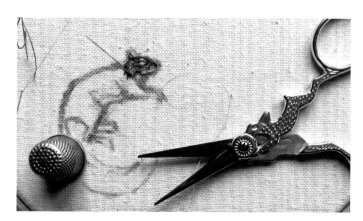

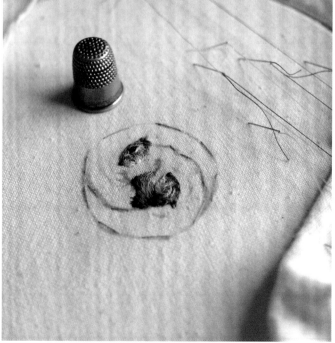

❧ 'Dormouse' ❧
2015

Finished in a 7.6cm (3in) hoop

· · · · · · · · · ·

Dormice are a subject I have been interested in from the beginning of my embroidery journey.

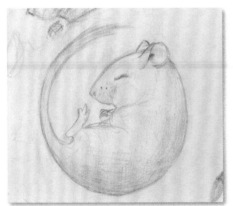 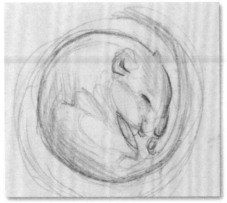 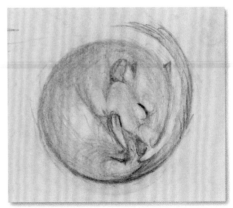

I have always been very taken with the idea of trying to capture the folds of a dormouse's fur when it curls up to sleep, first in pencil, then in thread. The rich gold fur against pink paws and nose make a beautiful colour combination that I adore.

I tried different ways of posing the dormouse, attempting to find the best method to portray the three-dimensional appearance I was aiming for.

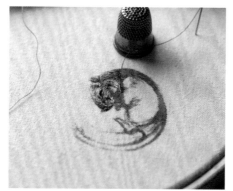

I have stitched several dormice over the years, each time doing something slightly new. My first dormouse was worked on undyed calico, as I had not started using fabric dye at that point. Usually when I return to the same animal I play with fabric colours, as I am more confident of the creature's contours and colours. However, when I revisited dormice later on I stuck with the calico's natural colour as I felt this best suited the gentle golds of the mice.

Getting the tones right in the fur was key. I had to be very aware of where the fur would be bunched along the contours of its tiny body, but also mindful of capturing the light in the real animal — where it would go into shadow as the fur tucked inwards.

I have always been fascinated by mustelids, and I had
sketched out several pine martens long before I took
the plunge and embroidered one. Their numbers in
England are still low, despite conservation work,
and I have never seen one with my own eyes in
the wild. For now, I have to live vicariously through
my embroideries!

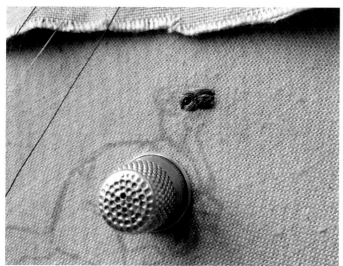

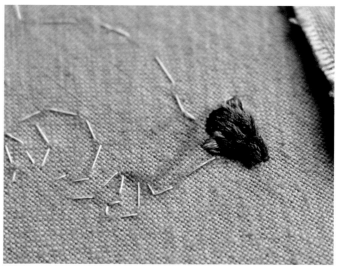

I selected a range of rich, dark browns for this piece: I wanted to avoid
using any browns with a greyish undertone, as I felt they would have dulled
the overall embroidery.

Pine martens have a very dense coat, particularly in winter, which was what
really drew me to them. It was also this thick coat that made me decide
to portray the marten in motion: there would be more movement and
contrast to show in the fur.

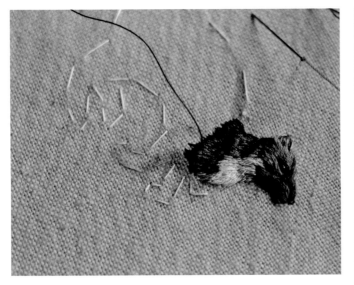

To portray the folds and ruffles of fur, I made sure to alternate between light and dark tones every time there was a shift in movement of the fur. I am normally very careful with blending lights and darks in my embroideries, but here it was important to not be afraid to push myself and create greater contrasts of highlights and shadows, in order to get the right effect.

I wanted a low-key background for this piece, as I was mostly interested in capturing the pine marten's rich dark fur. For this reason, although I spent some time looking at various plants for the flora, such as cloudberries, I eventually went for a simplified design with only leaves and berries.

• • • • • • • • • •

Approaching animals I do not normally embroider is always a
steep learning curve, so although I am pleased with the finished
piece I know I have got a lot more to learn. Here, I am aware I still
need to develop my technique to better convey how pine martens
and other mustelids move and appear. I know I will be returning to
them again and again in the future to further my understanding.

'Wolf Cub'

2018

Finished in a 15.25cm (6in) hoop

Despite always having an interest in wolves, I veered away from embroidering them for a long time. This was in part due to how often they appear in visual media, and I was not sure how to interpret them through my own ways of working.

. . . .

I was inspired to create this embroidery after doing a lot reading about the possibility of wolves being reintroduced to Scotland one day, so I did not want to default to a cold and intimidating representation. I found that approaching the animal as a cub made it easier, as they are much smaller and more endearing at that stage!

I wanted to avoid accidentally making the cub look like a dog, so in the sketchbook stage I focused on what would differentiate the two – in particular, I noted the wolf's larger paws and a broader face.

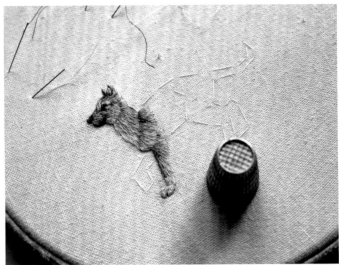

Colour selection is always a bit more difficult when you are embroidering something for the first time. It is not always easy to guess how colours will look together in the final piece. For this wolf, I wanted to capture a selection of warm tones mixed with greys, so I chose a range of creams and golds for the base coat, and then two greys that I interspersed as I worked to give the coat a more mottled appearance.

Overall, I am happy with the completed embroidery! I learned a huge amount about how to portray the wolf's most identifiable features, especially her multi-layered coat; it was unlike anything I had stitched before.

The idea of embroidering an adult wolf is still a challenging one to consider, but it definitely feels less intimidating now!

❦ 'Weasel' ❦

2018

Finished in a 10cm (4in) hoop

• • • • • • • • • • •

Despite their diminutive size (the 'common' or 'least' species range between 12.75–25cm / 5–10in), weasels are ferocious predators capable of killing rabbits, chickens and various rodents, and they have even been known to attack hares.
It was this fierce reputation that inspired me to pair this weasel with a rabbit skull.

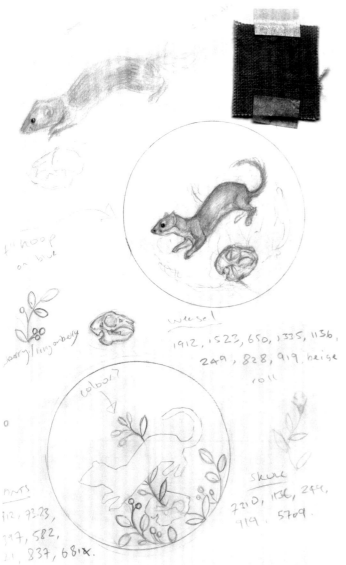

f'' hoop
on blue

berry/lingonberry

weasel
1912, 1523, 650, 1335, 1136,
249, 828, 919, beige
roll

colour?

skull
7310, 1136, 244,
919, 5709.

ANTS
312, 7323,
347, 582,
11, 837, 681x.

Blue is my favourite fabric colour to work on as I find it contrasts
brilliantly with the colour palettes I like to use for my work;
in this case, the rich oranges of the weasel's coat and the bright red
in the lingonberries.

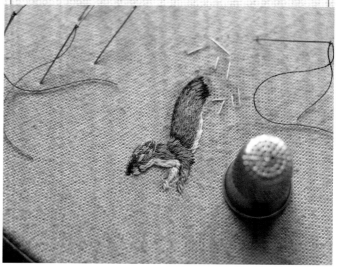

I always begin with the animal that is the focus of the embroidery and
then work the rest of the details in around it. This is because I am
quite prone to changing my mind in how I stitch the animal as I go. This
is often only in very small ways, such as moving the angle of a limb or
where a tail curves, but it can affect the look of a whole embroidery.
This order allows me to rework parts of the background motifs and
help them sit better in the composition.

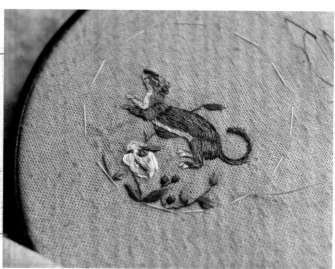

Finished in a 10cm (4in) hoop

Badgers are the most recent animal I have added
to my embroidery repertoire. I have always had
a soft spot for these beautiful, elusive creatures,
but they are not easy to re-create.

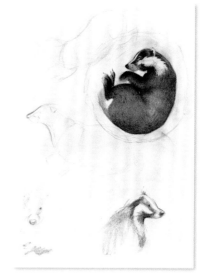

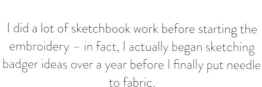

I did a lot of sketchbook work before starting the embroidery – in fact, I actually began sketching badger ideas over a year before I finally put needle to fabric.

Being less familiar with the behaviour of badgers, I wanted to gain an understanding of their basic structure and how they move; without this, I cannot create an accurate representation from my imagination. I also wanted to explore how to interpret their thick coats, as this covers most of the muscles I normally define in my embroideries to help give the animal a three-dimensional appearance.

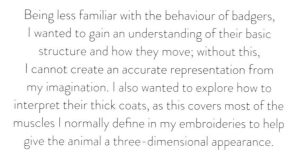

As I had decided to embroider a cub, I made sure to give the badger in my final sketch a smaller, more delicate body and a larger head to make it more youthful.

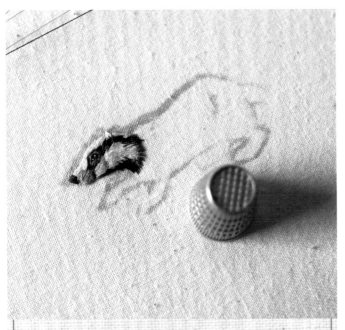

I began working very slowly at first. I needed to adjust to using greys instead of my usual warmer colours; I also had to keep making sure I worked to my original drawing, so the appearance of the badger would be accurate.

I tried to avoid using pure black and white threads as much as possible, as these can make an embroidery look flat. Most of the darker areas of this piece are actually done with a very dark purple, and I only used pure white for the eye highlights, everything else was done with a range of creams.

The background plants were comprised of branches of oak and rose hips, as well as some fly agaric mushrooms. I found all of these reds and oranges helped bring out the warmer tones in the badger, and brought its character to life.

Unlike most of my other work, I decided to stitch this badger on undyed calico as I felt the blacks, purples and greys would stand out well enough without the need for a bright background colour.

While looking through reference photos, I had noticed that badgers often have some warmer tones in their fur, over their stomach in particular; so, as well as selecting a range of darker threads, I picked out a pale beige to intersperse throughout the coat.

In the past, I have not liked the look of stitching mostly green plants on undyed calico. To avoid this here, I opted for more reds and oranges, creating an autumnal theme that I felt fitted well with the badger.

Once I had got the hang of using this colour palette, the embroidery flowed along quite easily. The main lesson I took from this piece was to go gently with the colour shifts in the bulk of the badger's coat, so as not to lose its voluminous, fluffy appearance. I am glad I resisted the urge to use a lot of black too, as I feel sticking to creams and warmer-hued greys makes the cub feel more lively.

This embroidery got me addicted to stitching badgers! I wound up with pages and pages of drawings, all of which I know will become embroideries one day!

'Skulls'
2016

Finished in 10cm (4in) hoops

• • • • • • • • • •

Over the years, I have spent a lot of time studying skulls in my sketchbook –
I find becoming familiar with the underlying structure of an animal makes it a lot
easier to understand and depict how the fur and muscles move later on. I wanted
to explore this interest further through embroidery, entwining it with themes
of life and rebirth that I often consider in my work. So, as my main subjects,
I selected fox and deer skulls to work with as they are animals that are almost
always present in my work.

. . . .

Working in my sketchbook allowed me to explore the differences between my two chosen skulls in greater detail – in particular, the powerful jaw and canines of the fox versus the large molars of the deer for chewing vegetation.

It is a bit harder to pick identifiable shapes when observing a skull compared to that of a live animal, and it is easy to get lost in the detail. Try to pick out the most obvious markers and focus on these, and leave out the smaller, less obvious elements to create a simple, overall impression of the skull. With the fox skull sketches shown right, I concentrated on the flowing line at the top of the skull, the shape of the eye socket and then the curve of the jaw; minor joints are hinted at through minor changes in tone.

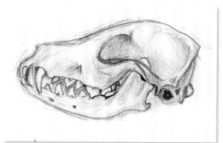

Tackling the skulls in profile makes the sketching process simpler and I believe creates a more striking silhouette. I try not to overwork the tones at this stage, as the background will be black and I do not want any part of the skulls to be too dark.

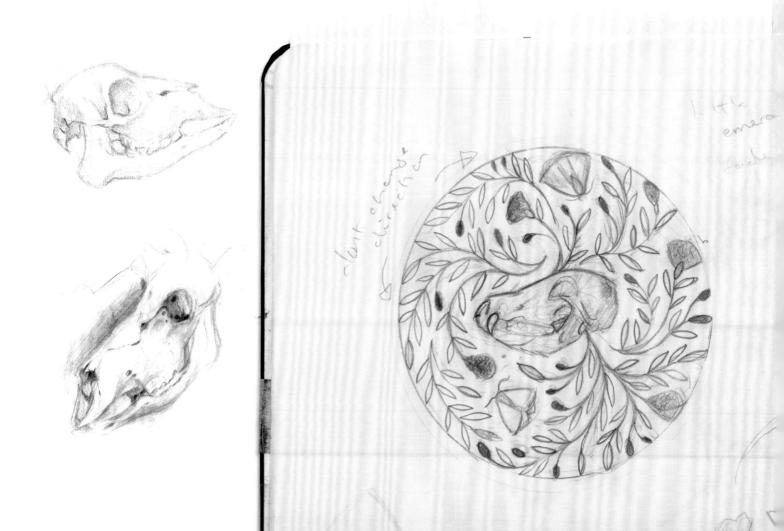

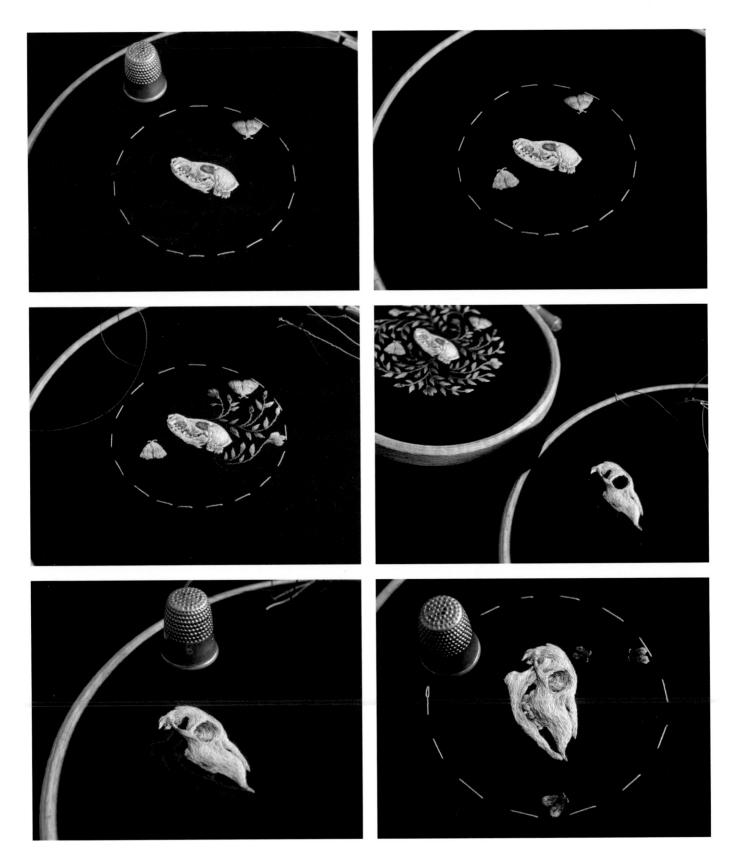

My main reason for deciding to work on black for these embroideries was to create a striking contrast between the fabric and skulls, as well as the plants. When I selected my thread palette, I wanted colours that were more vivid than the ones I usually used, so I picked out greens and blues that had a slight turquoise hue. To add a lively contrast to the sober nature of the piece, I added my favourite lepidopteran – the moth – to each of the compositions, stitching their wings with the same coloured threads as the flowers to make their presence more cohesive too.

I had to work slightly differently for this piece due to this colour scheme. I found I could not get a solid enough black by dyeing calico, so I opted for a pure black cotton instead. I also drew the design out with a chalk pencil so that it could be wiped off after finishing the embroidery – although chalk does tend to smudge easily throughout the stitching process.

. . . .

These pieces were my first foray into embroidering skulls, and they are something I have continued to incorporate into my work ever since. They are definitely more difficult to capture in embroidery work than my usual furry subjects, but I am happy to keep on wrangling with them as the final embroideries are worth the bother!

Development & evolution

Over the years, my backgrounds have, in general, become more complex. I'm very inspired by artworks like the tapestries of Edward Burne-Jones, in which he is able to include a huge amount of detail but still maintain a sense of depth. Unlike when painting, I can't use transparent layers or colour washes to build up an embroidery background, and I don't like to make backgrounds that are a solid block of stitching as it then competes with the animal, which is supposed to be the main focus. Instead, I have to rely on selecting the right colours and carefully arranging them to build up a scene. Although it would be quicker to do this digitally (and I do use Procreate® on my tablet to work out roughly what colours I will use) I prefer to draw my backgrounds out by hand and use layers of tracing paper to create the different layers and see how everything overlaps and interacts.

In the following chapter, I have included three of my most recent pieces of work, and will guide you through them step by step, to show you how I successfully build up my backgrounds and use them to complement my animals.

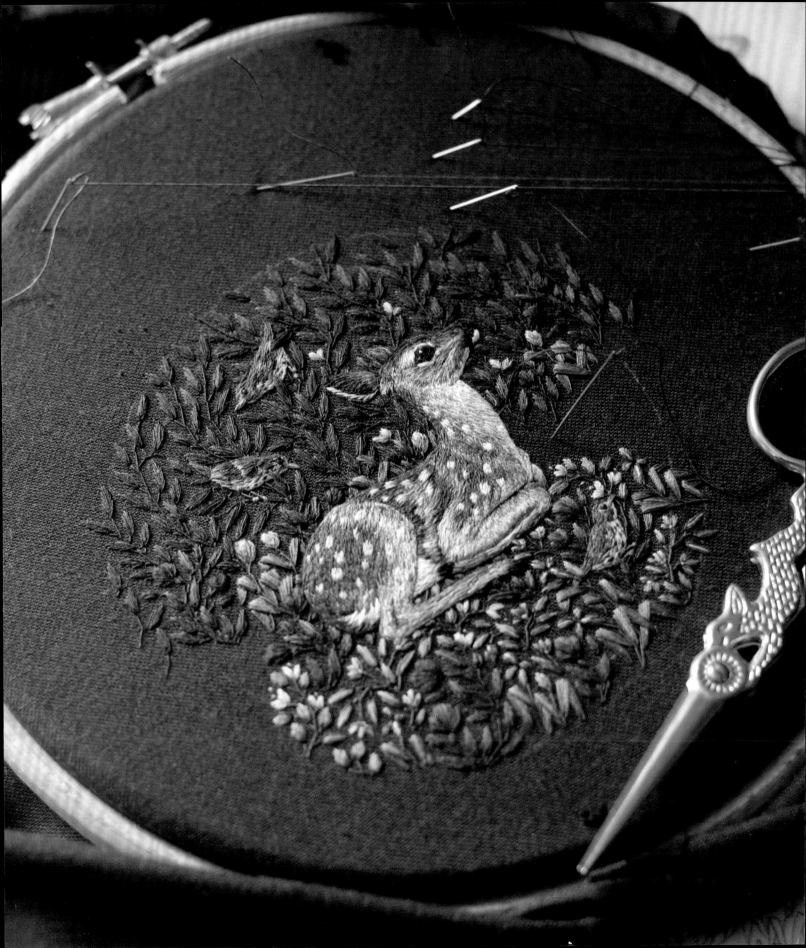

'Sleeping Fawn'

2021

Finished in a 10cm (4in) hoop

In this piece, I wanted to reimagine my 2014 sleeping fawn embroidery and see how I could integrate it into a more complex background design.

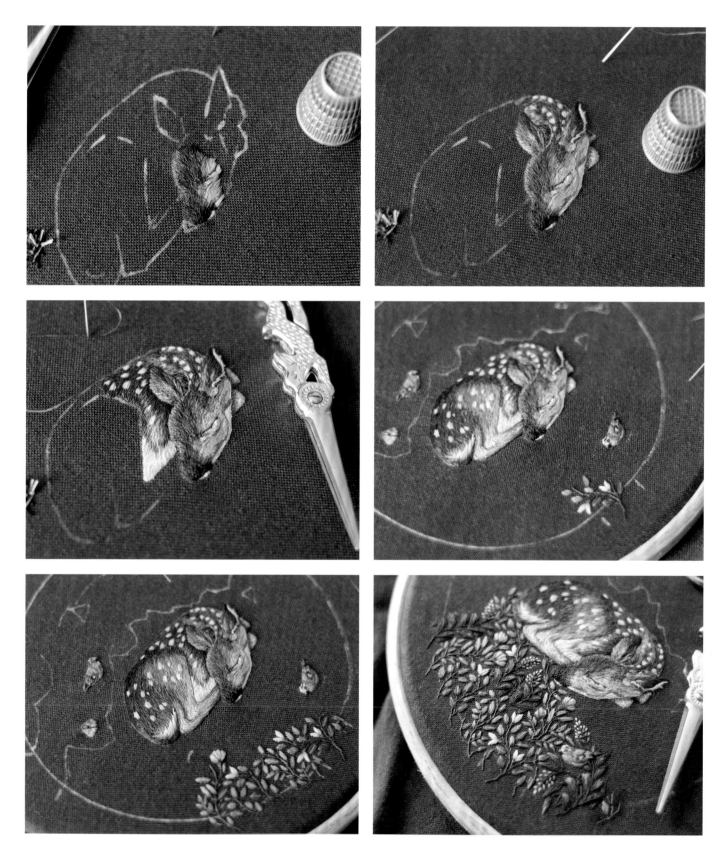

Using a rich variety of stitch textures, flower shapes and other wildlife gives the embroidery a huge amount of interest, allowing the eye to travel from one place to another and discover new things. However, the muted colours used and even placement of flowers means that overall, the background doesn't overpower the fawn.

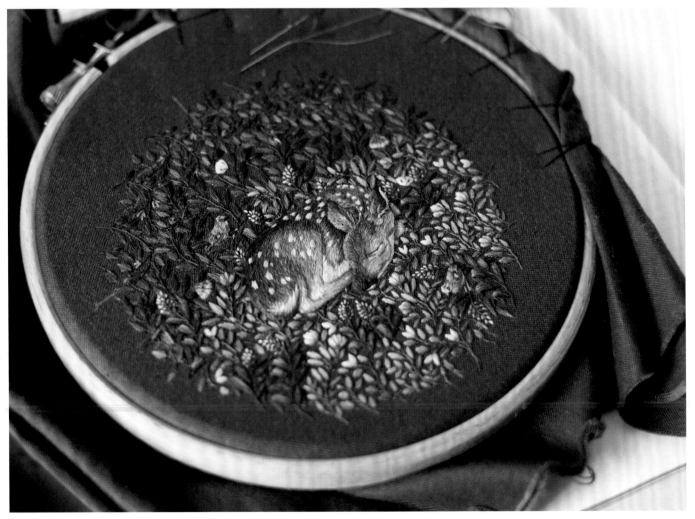

Quite often I will have a layer of very dark plants (almost the same colour as the fabric) as a base, then add one or two lighter layers overlapping it. These alternating areas of light and dark allow the eye a break from all the detail – if everything is bright and on the same layer it can be visually overwhelming and leave the viewer unable to focus on the areas you really want them to see. In this case, I wanted the focus on the fawn and the centre of the embroidery in general, so the line of lighter flowers suddenly switching to dark plants cuts through the centre of the design and draws the eye.

. . . .

'Fiat Lux'

2022

Finished in a 7.6cm (3in) hoop

· · · · · · · · · ·

In this design of a bright-eyed fawn alongside
song thrushes, I wanted to work in a range of
flowers and background details without losing
control of the overall composition.

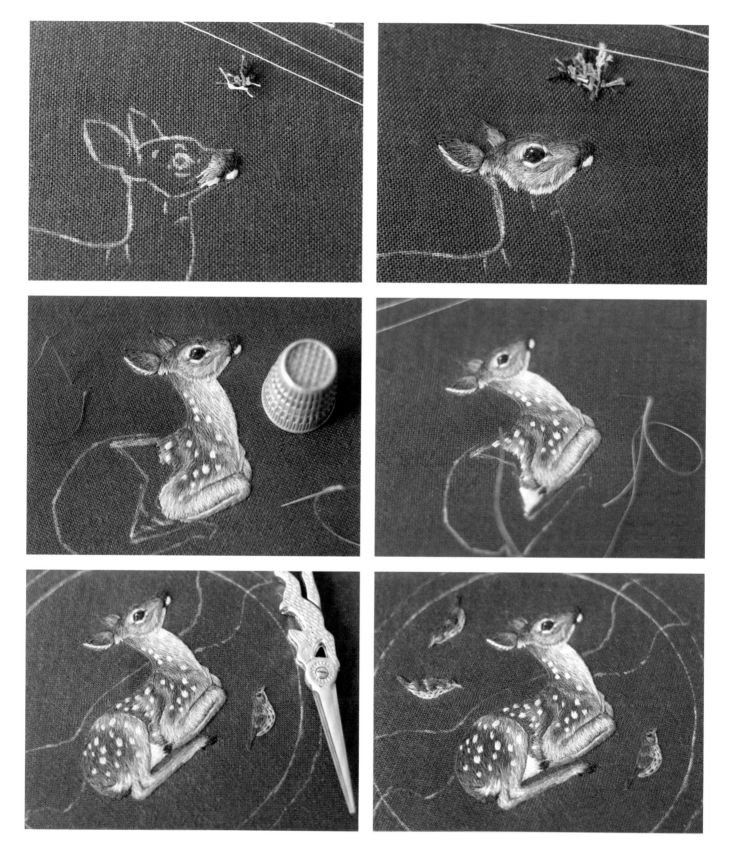

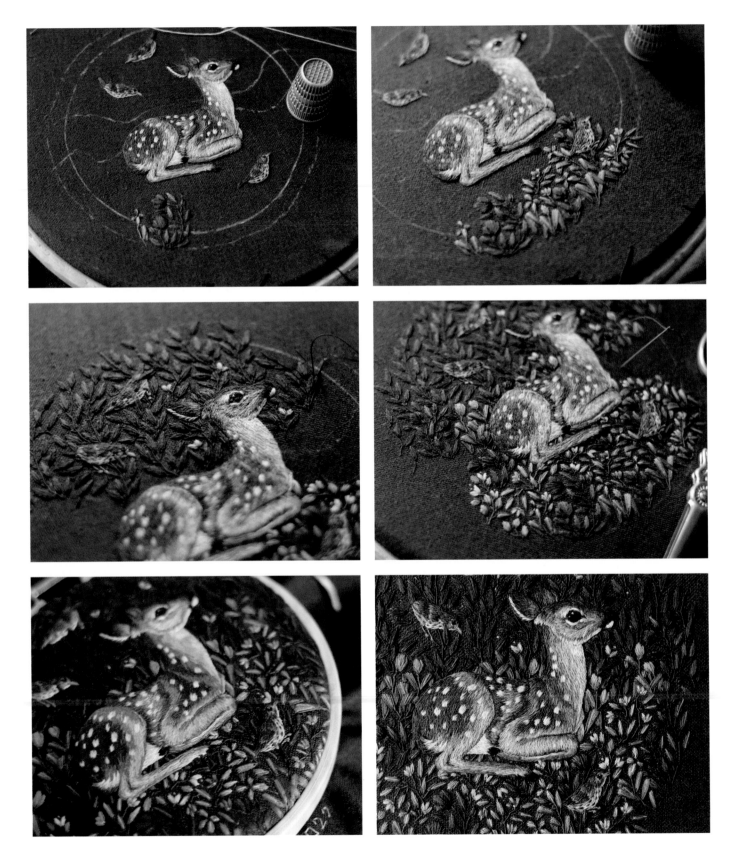

When designing this piece, I knew I wanted to include multiple flowers and birds, but didn't want to make the finished piece too crowded. To keep a handle on the different colours in use, I ordered the flowers into layers rather than mixing them all together. Starting at the bottom of the hoop there is a line of red, purple and blue; then switching to yellow and blue; then to red and pink – this final layer also used darker greens than the first two so it is slightly more muted. Underneath all of these is the dark green base layer, which only features a handful of yellow flowers around the fawn's head. For the birds, I kept to colours that are more muted than those of the fawn, so that they didn't 'pop' out too much.

When working on these more complex background designs, I've found separating everything into layers is vital to stop the composition from descending into chaos. I want to give the viewer's eye places to rest from the busier areas and to use these darker areas to bring attention to the focus of the embroidery – in this case, the fawn's head. I tend to not put any bright plants or background elements close to the animal's head so they don't distract from the detail there.

'Starry Messenger'

2023

Finished in a 10cm (4in) hoop

· · · · · · · · · ·

Returning once again to the hare motif, I wanted
to capture the magic of one dancing amongst
ghost moths and harebell flowers.

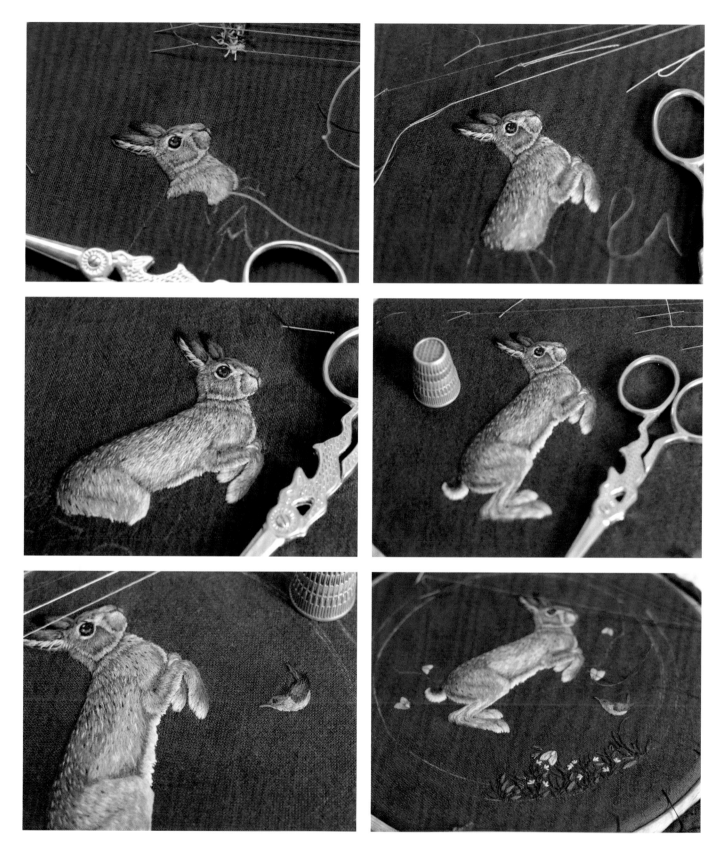

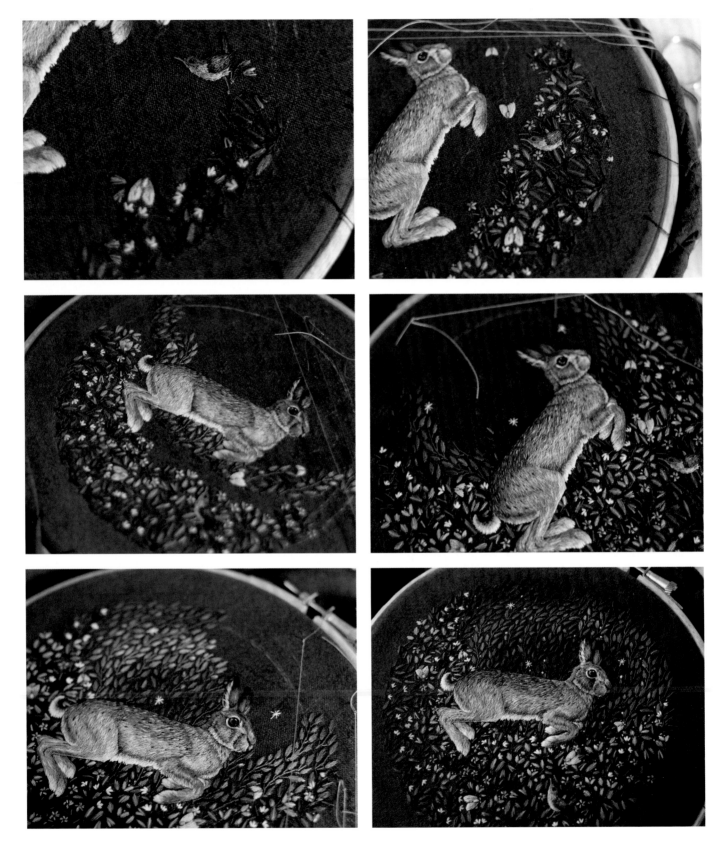

In this piece I wanted to include the sky as part of the background design but also stick with only using plants in the background, rather than solid blocks of stitching. To achieve this, I filled the sky with organic, leaf-like plant shapes in a range of blue tones. As well as using light blues that would stand out, I also picked some very dark blues that merged with the fabric colour underneath.

When deciding where I would place the blue tones, I made sure to keep the plant shapes around the hare's head dark, as lighter areas right next to it would compete with the hare; having a dark background behind it gives a rich texture to the background while keeping the focus in the right place.

. . . .

In the lower half of the embroidery I opted for purple harebells and blue-tinged meadow crane's-bill that would match the sky and background fabric, but also included the bird's-foot-trefoil to add sparks of gold throughout the piece.

Last word

Although I often get asked about my working process, I struggle to give a concise answer. My work consists of hours of studying and researching my animals, combined with decisions that are made on the go, so to summarize and articulate the way in which my embroideries are made is a difficult thing to do! I hope this book has succeeded in giving a thorough explanation of what I do and why I do it. My techniques and ideas are constantly evolving, and this extended edition aims to lay out the shifts in detail and design that have taken place in my work since the first edition of this book was published.

When I began studying to become an illustrator, I had never attempted embroidery (or any kind of sewing). Since picking up my first needle and length of thread, my work — in both style and focus — has gone through enormous changes. I hope, then, that this book can bring comfort to any readers who worry that they lack the knowledge or experience to jump into a new creative venture: with enough study and practice, it is possible to make new roads into any skill you wish to try out.

I could not have predicted the role embroidery now plays in my life. It has allowed me to work with an unrestrained creativity, without any preconceptions of how I should be doing things. I hope my story will inspire you to jump straight in and start trying out this medium if you have not already. Mistakes will happen every step of the way, but that is always the best way to learn.

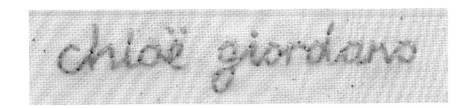

❧ About the author ❧

Chloe Giordano is regarded as one of the world's top embroiderers. She began to sew in the last year of her Illustration degree at the University of the West of England, and since graduating in 2011 she has continued to experiment with freehand embroidery, using sewing thread and hand-dyed fabrics. She has worked with a number of respected clients, including Vintage Books, Penguin and Bloomsbury.

Chloe has been featured on numerous textile art websites including Textile Artist (textileartist.org), Colossal (thisiscolossal.com), as well as Mary Corbet's Needle 'n Thread (needlenthread.com) and Bored Panda (boredpanda.com). Based in North Yorkshire, UK, she sells her original pieces, prints and greetings cards on Etsy and through her website: www.chloegiordano.com